UNCLE AL CAPONE

The Untold Story From Inside His Family

By Deirdre Marie Capone

"…Throughout the book, Capone tries to reconcile what she knows about her family with recorded history. Early in the book she writes, "I will not pretend to be able to paint a rosy picture of my uncle Al. I cannot make him out to be a perfect man, or even a good man. But what I want people to know is that he was a complex man. He was human and he had a heart." Capone succeeds, balancing both the public history of Al, from the Valentine's Day Massacre to his incarceration at Alcatraz, with personal photos, family recipes, and her own memories…It's not always an easy task as the author recounts losing friends, jobs, and other opportunities, once people learned she was a descendant of the notorious Al Capone… (it is) a memoir that is as complex and human as the man that it's about. It brings a fresh perspective to the other Al Capone biographies, and finally gives the larger-than-life gangster the one thing that may have eluded him in life: to be seen as simply a human being." *Katerie Prior, ForeWord Reviews:*

R Recap Publishing Co.

ISBN: 0982845103
ISBN-13: 9780982845103
LCCN: 2010911023

Al Capone & Deirdre Marie

Dedication

I dedicate this book to the family Capone that I knew and loved and who knew and loved me, most importantly my father Ralph Gabriel Capone. My hope is that my life and success will give his short life some real meaning.

Acknowledgments

Over the course of writing this book which began in the 1950s there have been many people who have listened, talked, and encouraged me to move forward sometimes through the tears I was shedding.

First I will start with my husband Bob. He was the first person in my life who did not judge me or criticize me because I was a Capone. I met him in 1957 working at the same insurance company who fired me because of my name. We lost each other for a couple of years but then found each other and picked up our romance where we left it. He is my best friend and partner. He helped me more than anyone, with this project. He put in many, many hours, helping me research the facts and proofreading. Thank you Honey!

Other people who deserve my thanks are Chuck Pipher my computer guru and friend and his wife Jackie for lending him to me for so many hours.

My son Jeff for taking so much of his valuable time to read my chapters, look over contracts and make suggestions, and my other three children for their support and encouragement.

Foreword

When word got out that I was writing this book I was bombarded with questions about it. One of the most frequent questions I encountered was "Is your book any different than the many other books written about Al Capone"?

The answer was always an emphatic "Yes"!

Granted, there have been many good books written about Uncle Al, but they all have one thing in common: none of the authors actually knew the man. They relied primarily on previous books, newspaper articles, and government records.

This is the only book written about Al by someone from inside his family, someone who as a little girl sat on his lap, hugged and kissed him, and traded "knock-knock" jokes with him.

Someone who helped him cook spaghetti, ate many meals with him and slept in his house.

Someone whom he taught to swim, ride a bicycle, and play the mandolin.

And probably most importantly, someone who as an adult had countless conversations with his older brother and business partner (my grandfather Ralph) as well as his other brothers and his only sister.

Someone whose father was raised by Al's mother in Al's house.

Someone whose father committed suicide due to the burden of the Capone name.

Someone who was scorned by classmates for many years, and was fired from jobs because she was related to Al Capone.

Only in this book will you find previously unpublished family photos and mouthwatering authentic Capone family recipes.

I promise you, Dear Reader, that after reading this book you will know things about Al Capone and his family that none of his biographers ever knew.

Table Of Contents

"THERE'S A LOT OF PEOPLE IN CHICAGO THAT HAVE GOT ME PEGGED FOR ONE OF THOSE BLOODTHIRSTY MOBSTERS YOU READ ABOUT IN STORYBOOKS. THE KIND THAT TORTURES HIS VICTIMS, CUTS OFF THEIR EARS, PUTS OUT THEIR EYES WITH A RED-HOT POKER AND GRINS WHILE HE'S DOING IT. NOW GET ME RIGHT. I'M NOT POSING AS A MODEL FOR YOUTH. I'VE HAD TO DO A LOT OF THINGS I DON'T LIKE TO DO. BUT I'M NOT AS BLACK AS I'M PAINTED. I'M HUMAN. I'VE GOT A HEART IN ME."......AL CAPONE

1

I Don't Like Mustard,
and I Am Related To Al Capone

I have always been opposed to violence, to shootings. I have fought, yes, but fought for peace. And I believe I can take credit for the peace that now exists in the racket game in Chicago. I believe that the people can thank me for the fact that gang killings here are probably a thing of the past.
- Al Capone

I am a Capone. My grandfather was Ralph Capone, listed in 1930 as Public Enemy #3 by the Chicago Crime Commission. That makes me the grand niece of his partner and younger brother, Public Enemy #1: Al Capone.

For much of my life, this was not information that I readily volunteered. In fact, I made every effort to hide the fact that I was a Capone, a name that had brought endless heartache to so many members of my family. In 1972, when I was in my early thirties, I left Chicago and my family history far behind me, reinventing myself in Minnesota and making sure that no one in my life other than my husband Bob knew my ancestry. I succeeded— even with our four children.

But the truth about who I was hovered at the edges of the reality I had created, and I was terrified of it—terrified of revisiting the shy, wounded girl who grew up friendless, shunned by classmates, forbidden to play with a mobster's child; terrified of once again hearing those dreaded words, "You're fired," and seeing another employer's doors close to me because of my name; terrified of reawakening the grief of losing both my father and brother to suicide, collateral damage of the Capone legacy; and, above all, terrified that if my children learned they had "gangster blood" running through their veins, they'd be exposed to the same pain I had experienced.

As if this weren't enough, my silence was also motivated by a little trick of fate truly stranger than fiction. My husband's uncle married the sister of one of the men killed in the St. Valentine's Day Massacre. As you'll read later in this book, I have good reason to believe that Al Capone was not as responsible for those cold-blooded murders as history has written, but all the same, how could I bring such a terrible complication into our family life? How could I know that my aunt by marriage wouldn't see her brother's murderers in my face? This concern was overshadowed because I was more afraid of my children finding out about their ancestry so I kept up the false front.

When my nine-year-old son Bobby came home from school one day in 1974 to announce that his class was learning about Al Capone, it knocked the wind out of me.

Ever since my children started school, I had developed the habit of asking, "What did you learn today?" when they came home. Of course, I always listened to their answers with great interest, but on that particular day, I felt like the whole world had just slid out of focus, leaving only Bobby and me. There he was, smiling and cheerful as always, telling me he was learning about my uncle in his fourth grade class.

My heart seized, but somehow, I managed to get out a half-casual, "What did you learn about Al Capone?" "We learned that he was a gangster," Bobby told me. He went on to tell me about Prohibition in the 1920s and 30s, Al's bootlegging operation, and how he had been such an expert outlaw that when the police finally nabbed him, the only charge they could pin on him was tax evasion. I was so astonished that all I could do was nod along as he spoke.

Later that evening, when Bob and I were alone, I told him what Bobby had said. I felt like I had been holding my breath ever since Bobby so innocently chirped the name "Capone." Bob and I decided together that we couldn't keep the truth from our children any longer. We had no idea how they would react, but one thing was certain—we didn't want them to hear about it from someone else, and now that our oldest kids were teenagers, they had started to ask about their grandparents. We couldn't keep this from them forever.

The next evening, as Bob and I gathered our kids in the kitchen, I was petrified. This was a moment I had created in my head time and again, since Bob and I decided to start a family. And each time I imagined it, it ended badly. I thought our kids would be furious with me for keeping the secret, or for even being a Capone in the first place. Maybe they would be ashamed of me. Or worse yet—maybe they would be ashamed of themselves. Maybe hearing the truth about their family would send them into the same kind of downward spiral that had swallowed so much of my childhood.

When I was growing up, I was often mad at God for making me a Capone. I couldn't understand why other children weren't allowed to play with me, and my heart broke every time I heard someone murmur a slur or read the newspapers' awful accusations about the family I loved—and the family that loved me in return while everyone else shunned me. If these were my prevailing memories of growing up as a Capone, I just couldn't imagine that things would be any different for my children. As I sat them down at the kitchen table and prepared to break the news, I felt like I was on the verge of crushing the happy life that Bob and I worked so hard to give to them.

I could tell they sensed my nervousness, and they sat unusually quiet as I told them I had something important to say. I squeezed Bob's hand tightly, and the words came slowly.

"There's something I want to tell you about my family," I began. "Al Capone was my uncle. My grandfather was his brother. I was born Deirdre Marie Capone."

For a split second, there was silence in the kitchen. I could feel my heart in my throat. Then, at the exact same instant, all four of my children in unison exclaimed, "Cool Mom!"

In retrospect, I suppose I should have anticipated the reaction, think about what any teenager might say upon hearing they are related to a legend. But to be honest, their excitement was the last thing in the world that I expected. I was so used to hiding and living in quiet shame that it just didn't cross my mind that my children might be more intrigued than upset.

But of course, it was a different time. I grew up with headlines about the menace of Al Capone's "Outfit" splashed across the front page. I grew up seeing my classmates' parents look at me and my family with constant suspicion and fear. I grew up well accustomed to men in dark suits guarding the Capone family home with machine guns. My children, on the other hand, grew up thinking of Al Capone as a celebrity, a folk hero more than a criminal.

As soon as that word, "Cool!" broke the tension in the room, the two younger kids chimed in. Bobby's eyes grew wide as saucers and, before I knew it, all four of them were peppering me with questions. "What was he like? Was he nice to you? Did he love you? Do you look like him? Do you have pictures?"

Relief washed over me. I had built this moment up in my mind for so many years, but here I was, discovering that the very source of my shame was now the source of pride for my children. I tried to answer their questions as best I could. I pulled out my family photo albums and began to introduce my own children to the people who loved me most when I was their age.

First, there was Theresa Capone, the mother to Al and my grandfather. She was the rock of the Capones, the woman who held the family together as they emigrated from Italy to New York and then to Chicago. She had known poverty in Brooklyn and the realization of the "American Dream" as Al built his business in Chicago. She raised my father when his biological mother abandoned him, and she acted as a grandmother to me. Her house on Prairie Avenue became the warmest place in the world to me, even with heavy drapes drawn across the windows and armed men stationed at the doors.

Then there were her children. Mafalda—or, to me, Aunt Maffie—was the youngest and the only daughter. Only five years older than my dad, she was more of a sister to him than an aunt. To me, she was a hero and I was her spitting image. Everyone in the family called me "Little Mafalda."

The older children were six boys: Vincenzo, my grandfather Ralph and his younger brothers, Frank, Al, Mimi, Bites, and Matty. Frank, Ralph, and Al were all involved, to a greater or lesser extent, in earning the family's keep—which meant operating the Outfit, the organization that distributed liquor illegally during Prohibition. But to me, they were as far from "criminals" as anyone could get. They were loving, funny, larger-than-life men and fiercely proud of me. I could never reconcile the frightening images the newspapers painted of them with the warm-hearted people who teased and joked with me at Sunday dinners.

Finally, there was my dad, Ralph Gabriel Capone. In his short life, he had been the star and the hope of the family. He was keenly intelligent and determined to set out on a different path than his father and uncles. He wanted to make a name for himself with a legitimate business, but the Capone name dogged him and dashed his hopes. Ultimately, he took his own life when I was only ten years old.

Sitting at the table with my children and sharing these memories, some painful and some brimming with joy, was a defining moment for me. For many years, I had delved privately into my family's history, searching for the line between rumor and truth, and, very slowly, began shedding the thick blanket of shame that came with the Capone notoriety. But to offer this history to my children and to find that they were proud to call it their own was a new step for me. At the age of thirty-four, with the help of my children, I finally accepted myself as Deirdre Marie Capone.

Not only were my children happy to learn of their family ties to Al Capone, they loved to tell people about them. And today, I have fourteen grandchildren who all think of their heritage as a badge of honor. When my granddaughter, Abby, was in the second grade, her teacher made a book for the class in which each student wrote two things about themselves, something true and something untrue, so that the other children could guess which was which. Abby proudly wrote, "I don't like mustard" and "I am Al Capone's grand-grand-grand niece."

Deirdre Marie at 17

Long before I told my children about my family—in fact, long before I even had children—I began to research the Capone history. The research I did—sometimes by reading secondhand historical accounts, but more often by tapping the memories of the family members who lived that history personally—forms the basis of this book. It was my children's acceptance that gave me the courage to go ahead with the writing, but this book has been in the making for many years. In a sense, I have been writing this book all my life.

There was one episode in particular, when I was only seventeen, that set off my need to understand my family. In the fall of 1957, just after I graduated from high school, I got my first full-time job with an insurance company on LaSalle Street in Chicago. I was offered a full-ride scholarship to go to college, but my mother needed help supporting herself and my younger brother. The job was nothing glamorous; I earned $200 a month as a secretary in the Boiler and Machinery Division. Each week, I turned my entire check over to my mother.

At first, the job was not what I envisioned for myself, but over time, I began to adapt. I was proud of myself; I was never late, and I worked hard. My boss even suggested I take on stenographic work for him in addition to my regular duties. And I made friends there—in fact, it was at that company where I met Bob, my future husband.

So, when my boss called me into his office slightly more than six months into my stint there, I had no reason to believe he would have anything negative to say. I assumed he wanted to test my dictation skills, as he had done once before, so I brought my stenographic tablet with me into the office. He gestured at the chair across from his desk and asked me to have a seat. I, still suspecting nothing, sat down and got ready to take notes. But then he said something unexpected. "Deirdre, please tell me your name."

As soon as the words left his mouth, I felt my face flush and my heart begin to pound. There is a trait that runs in the Capone family: intuition. My uncle Al survived countless attempts on his life because of it. In fact, he even had premonitions in dreams that saved his life. And in that moment, sitting across from my boss, I sensed what was going to happen.

"Deirdre," I answered. "My name is Deirdre Gabriel."

For years, I had been going by Gabriel, my great-grandfather's first name and my father's middle name. My mother had even legally changed my brother's name from Ralph Capone to Ralph Gabriel, but she said it wasn't worth all the paperwork to change mine because I would get married someday and it would change then.

But my legal name did matter. I applied for the job as Deirdre Gabriel, and that's how everyone I worked with knew me. But because it was a life insurance company, I was eligible after six months for a free policy, and I had to use my legal name on the paperwork. As soon as that paperwork crossed his desk, the life insurance agent called my boss with the news.

"Tell me your real name," my boss said.

I swallowed. There was no sense trying to pretend. "Capone…Deirdre Marie Capone."

"Are you any relation to Al Capone?" He asked.

"Yes," I admitted, "he was my uncle."

For a moment, the words hung in the air between us. Then my boss sighed and shook his head. "I'm sorry," he said, "but we can't have you working here. I'm going to have to let you go. You're fired."

I don't know how I managed to get out of his office and into the ladies' room without breaking down, but somehow I found myself there, sobbing uncontrollably. By that time, Al Capone had been dead for ten years, and the Outfit was now run by Tony Accardo. But it was still associated with my family. It was just at that time in the 1950s that they began laundering money by investing it in legitimate businesses like insurance companies and car dealerships, then sitting on their boards. I realize in retrospect that the executives of the company I worked for worried that, by employing me, they might give law enforcement the false impression that the Outfit's money was behind their operations.

That was why they let me go. But at the time, even if I understood their logic, it wouldn't have offered consolation. As I cried in the ladies' room, I was overcome with shame. My being fired had nothing to do with my performance—I knew I had done a good job. And I saw this same situation destroy my father. He was enormously gifted, brimming with potential, but time and again, the Capone name had shut him out of opportunities. No matter what his merits, no matter how hard he worked, he couldn't get a leg up, and ultimately, those continual disappointments killed him.

And I had to wonder if the same thing would happen to me. I felt like the door to my true identity had suddenly flung open for all the world to see. A sinking feeling in my heart told me that if I was a Capone, I didn't deserve a nice job. I came from a bad family, and I was a bad person by association. I didn't deserve to sit across from an important man in a corner office with the sun shining through enormous windows. My real self finally caught up to me, and I understood that no matter what I did, I would always be doomed.

Somehow, I managed to regain my composure, clean out my desk, and leave the building. I got on the Illinois Central to go home, and the train's rhythmic chugging sounded like, "You're fired. You're fired. You're fired." I was sure everyone else in the train car could hear the same words. I felt like they were staring at me, the poor unemployed girl, punished for the sins of her family. I don't think the term "self-image" had been coined yet, but mine had taken a mighty blow.

The moment I got home, I knew exactly who to turn to. I called the woman who had always been my role model and confessor, my aunt, Maffie.

When I told her what happened, she answered without hesitating. "Come over and we'll talk about it," she said. "Uncle Johnny's working, and I could use the company. I'll fix us a good dinner of gravy and meatballs."

Though Maffie was technically my great-aunt, that label didn't hold much meaning in our family. The Capone generations were unusually blurred and interwoven. Because my father and Maffie were so close in age, they were much more like brother and sister than nephew and aunt. So, I considered Maffie my aunt and not my great-aunt.

This blurring of generations is partly why Maffie and I became so close. Add that to the fact that I, just like her, was the only Capone girl of my generation, and she treated me like someone special. Growing up, I spent a lot of time with her—often more than with my own mother. After my father died, she took me to my grandfather Ralph's place and we spent the whole summer there together, healing and reconnecting to family. When I became a teenager, she took me shopping, fixed my hair, and, along with my grandmother Theresa, taught me to cook all the intoxicating, authentic Capone family recipes.

Whenever I felt blue or had a personal problem, I'd turn to Maffie. I knew she would take my side—the Capone side. In fact, after I left my first husband, an abusive man who threatened our infant daughter, Maffie asked me if I wanted to have him killed. I politely declined, but I've always believed she would have arranged it if I had just said the word.

And so, naturally, I went to her when I got fired. She had the grit to deal with any blow to the family honor. When she was born in Brooklyn in 1912, her parents Gabriel and Theresa Capone named her after the ten-year-old princess of Italy, the second child of King Emmanuel III. It was the right choice. As the only living girl of nine children, Aunt Maffie was the princess of the Capone family, and she had no trouble handling the role. Her brothers spoiled her, and she in turn developed a sense of entitlement and a ferocious tongue that she didn't hesitate to use against anyone who crossed her or the people she loved. Everyone, myself included, was a little afraid of Maffie. She was the only member of the family I ever heard talk back to her mother, the matriarch Theresa.

Maffie was the female Al Capone. She had the dark, curly Capone hair that framed her wide-set eyes. But even with large hands, full eyebrows that almost met in the middle, and a habit of speaking through her teeth, there was something very feminine and attractive about her. She had both Al's courage and his temper, along with the "Al Capone stare." He was famous for it. All of a sudden, if he was threatened or in a tense situation, his face would just go stoic, and he would stare right through whatever hapless person crossed him. Aunt Maffie had the same focused, piercing stare.

She was fiercely proud of the Capone family name, and she was quick to defend her brother Al, even after he was sent to prison. Most of us, including Al's own son, took on other identities to escape the burden of the family name. But not Maffie. I still remember visiting her in a nursing home shortly before she died. She leaned into me and whispered, "Tell them who we are. Tell them we're Capones. They'll treat me better." She was one of the very few in our family who insisted that her real last name be marked on her headstone.

But Maffie's grit didn't only come from carrying Capone stock. It was also something she had to develop by necessity. She didn't have an easy life, something I witnessed firsthand. She was barely eighteen years old when she married Johnny Maritote, a creepy, charmless man who could never hope to match her. It was an arranged marriage, designed by Al to secure relations between members of the Outfit. Johnny was the younger brother of Frank Maritote (alias Frank Diamond), a ruthless, out-of-control member of Al's organization who was later killed by a shotgun blast.

Maffie told me that, as a little girl, she always dreamed of a big wedding but never had many suitors, much less proposals. As she put it, "Who would want to date Al Capone's little sister? You'd have to be crazy!" So, Johnny was Maffie's only chance. But while the marriage was good for business, and gave the Outfit reason to hope Frank Diamond would be held in check, Uncle Al was never happy about it. He knew both Maritote brothers were thugs. And that was the real reason he didn't attend Maffie's wedding—

not, as was reported, because he was afraid of being arrested or attacked at such a public event.

Al, however, did agree to pay for the wedding. How could he deny his baby sister the day of her dreams? He spent extravagantly, inviting four-thousand guests, including most of the Raiola family in Italy. Maffie loved to describe the occasion to me. In fact, in her house, she kept a photograph on the wall of the wedding cake. It was nine feet long and four feet high and baked in the shape of a ship—just like the cruise ship that Al would send them on for their honeymoon. The cost of the cake alone was $2,100—in 1930 dollars! And the cake paled in comparison to the wedding gown. Maffie wore an ivory satin dress with a twenty-five-foot train. It took four women to hold the train up as she walked down the church aisle.

But, unfortunately for Maffie, the wedding was the best part of her marriage. After that gorgeous ceremony, her union with Johnny never brought her joy. I never heard them say a single affectionate word to each other. Johnny was a brooding man who gave me the creeps. Once when I was thirteen and stayed overnight at their house, I noticed him spying on me as I undressed. That same summer, at the Capone compound in Wisconsin, he offered to give me a driving lesson and insisted I sit on his lap. He began making inappropriate comments and movements. After that, I tried to stay as far away from him as possible.

In 1975, after I had been out of touch with all of the Capones for almost a decade, I called Aunt Maffie to say hello. Uncle Johnny answered the phone and gave me an enthusiastic, "Deirdre, where have you been? We've missed you!" I told him honestly that that was hard to believe—I didn't think he loved me. His response was: "If I didn't love you so much, I would have raped you when you were thirteen." What kind of a man would say something like that? If I had had any doubts before, those words confirmed that my aunt Maffie had gotten a bad deal in that arranged marriage.

However, it was Johnny who finally drove home to me how much my aunt had cared about me. After she passed away in 1988, my husband Bob, our youngest son Jeff, and I all paid our respects to Johnny at his home in Michigan, where he and Maffie had moved to be closer to their daughter and granddaughter. He was happy to see us, and said over and over how much Aunt Maffie loved me and always called me "Little Mafalda." He showed us a baby picture of me, which Maffie had displayed on her bedroom dresser for half a century. Seeing that photo sent a little wave of pain through me. Maffie's later years coincided with the time when I needed to separate myself from being a Capone, and I had fallen out of touch with her. But, still, nothing could diminish the tremendous role Maffie played in my life—and how, on that day in 1957 when I lost my job, she instilled in me a new sense of pride in our family.

Deirdre Marie at 9 months

When she opened the door to me that afternoon, the first thing she did was give me a fierce, tight hug of sympathy. Then, she unleashed a slew of choice words about my boss. But I was only seventeen and felt scared and sorry for myself. In my sorrow, I blurted, "Aunt Maffie, why did Uncle Al do so many bad things? Why was he such a terrible person?"

Aunt Maffie's face crumpled. I could tell by the look in her eyes that I had broken her heart. She stared at me with a mixture of surprise and pain, as if my words were a dagger that I had shoved in her heart. Her face seemed to say, "I thought I would never hear those words come from your mouth."

For a brief moment, tears actually sprang to her eyes. But then she rallied. Her teeth came together, and her fists clenched at her sides. This was the Maffie we were all in awe of—this was the Maffie who could pierce anyone with her eyes. She grabbed me by the arms and sat me on the sofa. Sitting down next to me, she said in a firm voice, through her teeth, "Look, if you want to be mad at someone, be mad at the idiot who fired you."

Her eyes left mine briefly and she seemed to be searching her memory, trying to find the words to make me understand her fierce loyalty to the family. Then, that stare locked onto me once again.

"My big brother, Al, was the man who kept our family together when my father died," she told me. "I was only eight years old. We had no means, and Al became the chief breadwinner. He moved the whole family— including your dad, who was just a baby—from Brooklyn to Chicago. If it hadn't been for him, we would all have starved."

Aunt Maffie went on to try to get me to understand what the culture had been like in the 20s and 30s, when Prohibition was an almost universally unpopular law. "Deirdre, it was a business," she said matter-of-factly. "The government was telling people they couldn't drink, but people wanted to drink. So, the businessmen who supplied alcohol were filling a need. The Kennedys did it. The Rockefellers did too. And Al and your grandfather… they were supplying high quality stuff; it wasn't rotgut. They were giving the people what they wanted, and the people loved them for it. Al's speakeasies were full of politicians, police officers, judges—I saw them there myself. They were his best customers, and half of them were on his payroll! He wasn't some ruthless person, committing crimes for sport. He was a businessman. And then, Prohibition was overturned, and the 'crimes' people wanted to hang him for became perfectly legal and honorable."

Maffie went on to tell me that she knew Al as well as anyone, and she would lay down her life on the fact that he never peddled drugs or intentionally harmed a single innocent person.

For a moment, I hesitated. "What about the people the Outfit killed?" I asked quietly.

Maffie nodded. "I knew you'd wonder about that," she said. "But you remember what we've always taught you. Family is everything. There were people out there who were trying to kill Al for their own gain— because he was the biggest competition there was. And they were willing to go so far as to threaten his family. When you were just a little girl, some of them were willing to threaten you. That's where Al drew the line. He didn't tolerate backstabbing, and he didn't tolerate people who wanted to hurt us."

She paused and held my gaze. I knew if there were ever a time to listen up, this was it. "No one in our family was ever involved in any cold-blooded killing," she said. "If somebody is trying to hurt you, aren't you permitted to protect yourself?"

Then she told me that she never knew a "gangster" who helped other people as much as Uncle Al. After the 1929 stock market crash, he set up soup kitchens all over Chicago and fed thousands of men, women, and children who otherwise would have starved. His speakeasies created jobs for people out of work and supported the careers of dozens of minority jazz musicians who perfected their craft performing for his customers.

"And my brother's word was his bond," Aunt Maffie finished. "Everyone knew that. He would have given his life to save your life or mine. So don't be so hard on him. He loved his family. He loved you. Don't you ever forget that, OK? Capish?"

That evening was a turning point in my life. Being a Capone had already influenced so much of who I was, but most of that influence centered on shame. Now, I wanted to understand my uncle Al and his partner, my grandfather Ralph, as human beings and not as "public enemies."

But much of their story took place before I was born. I was born in 1940, but Al and Ralph were at the height of their power during the 1920s. When I knew Al, he had already suffered through the seven-year imprisonment—most of it in Alcatraz—that changed him forever. And he died in 1947, when I was just a little girl.

So, to understand my family, I had to develop a strategy. From the day I was fired, I began to ask each member of my family—Aunt Maffie; my grandfather Ralph; Al's other brothers, Mimi, Bites, and Matty; Uncle Al's wife Mae, and their son Sonny—to tell me everything they would or could about Al and the family business. I wanted to know how things really were. What was the secret behind Al's business success? What was the true story of the St. Valentine's Day Massacre? What happened to Al in prison? And, of course, the question people have asked me all my life: Where did all the money go?

Some of my family members were more open than others, but all of them had stories to tell. And all of them were concerned that I might be writing a book. They made me promise that if I wrote anything, it would not be published until long after they were dead and buried.

At the end of his life, my father was in the process of writing a book about the family, which he called *Sins of the Father*. Just before he was found dead, Hedda Hopper mentioned in her gossip column that he was working on a manuscript. So, there was a lot of speculation in the years after his death that perhaps it wasn't suicide. Perhaps he had been murdered—not by any member of our family, but by some other member of either the Outfit or politics who was worried about being implicated with the Capones. I will tell the full story of the questions surrounding my father's death later in this book.

People have often asked me, "Why has no other member of the family ever written a book? Why didn't Sonny ever write a book?" I think it's because of the mystery that my dad's aborted manuscript created. In this book, I will tell what actually happened at the St. Valentine's Day Massacre—and who I believe were the real perpetrators—as well as many other, as of yet untold, stories about the inner workings of Capone's Outfit. Revealing these secrets is no small matter when you're a member of a family that had such ruthless and unscrupulous enemies. Even if my father wasn't murdered for working on a book, the fact that everyone believed he might have been is telling.

But now those unscrupulous enemies are long dead. And so, too, are all the members of my family who can remember Al Capone personally. Uncle Mimi, the last of Al's siblings, died in 1984. Sonny, Al's only child and my godfather, died in 2004. As far as I can tell, I am the last member of my family to be born with the Capone name. So now, finally, it is time for the story from inside the family to come to light.

I will not pretend to be able to paint a rosy picture of my uncle Al. I cannot make him out to be a perfect man, or even a good man. But what I want people to know is that he was a complex man. He was human—and he had a heart. He was a son, a brother, a father, and an uncle. There were two Al Capones. There was the Al Capone that strutted, wore fancy suits and big hats, and loved the limelight. There was the leader of the Outfit, who sat straight in his chair, stiff and rigid. The man who often wore a smile on his face that could instantly turn into an intimidating glare when he felt challenged.

And then there was the Al I knew—the man who would get on the floor and play with me like a big teddy bear; the man who would put on an apron and make spaghetti sauce, roaring with laughter the whole while; The man who would sing operettas in Italian at the top of his lungs and taught me to play the mandolin. This was the private Al Capone that no one ever saw. And this is the Al Capone who does not appear in the dozens of books you'll find about him. Professional biographers can tell you about the legend, the businessman, and the leader—which they do by researching old newspapers and police blotters—but only a member of his family can tell you about the man within.

And that's what I will do. I'll start at the beginning—in Italy in the late nineteenth century, when Al's parents were starting a family and deciding to come to America. And I'll tell you the family history from before I was born, the stories of Al and Ralph's bootlegging operation, and Al's imprisonment. Then I'll move forward in Al's life to tell you about the uncle I knew personally for seven years. And finally, I'll tell you about the legacy that Al left behind, what happened to me and the rest of the family after his death, and how we lived with both his memory and his legend. It is my hope that you will come to know Al as something more than an icon of an era. It is my hope that you will get a sense of him as a man.

Perhaps my most important reason for writing this book, however, is that I hope it will give my father's short life some meaning. It will finish the project of telling the Capone story that he began so many decades ago and was never able to complete. And it will, I hope, absolve him of the guilt he suffered from being the inheritor of the sins of his father. It will show that he came from a good family and produced a good family—mine.

If you read the biographies, you'll find no difference between the Capone boys and men like John Gotti. But I know that there was a difference—and I will share it with you in this book. I am a patriot because of the Capones. My love of this country—and my eagerness to contribute back to it—was instilled in me by the Capones. And I learned from the Capones what it means to have a warm, generous heart.

Have you ever wondered how two people can carefully follow the directions for a recipe, using the exact same ingredients and measurements, and achieve entirely different results? What happened? How could it be? It's a mystery. But I propose to solve that mystery. The solution can be reduced to one word: Love.

When the Capones taught me to cook, they taught me that cooking is a labor of love. My grandma Theresa used to say to me, with a little translation from Aunt Maffie, "When you cook for someone, you must do it with love in your heart. That makes everything taste better." How we think influences the outcome of what we do. Cook with love in your heart, and those you cook for will love the results.

On the evening after I was fired, Aunt Maffie brought me into her kitchen and taught me her famous meatball recipe. First, we ground the different meats—beef, veal, and pork—kneading them together with breadcrumbs, pine nuts, and Italian parsley. After molding them into balls, we fried them in lard, and once they were brown on all sides, we baked them in the oven, giving us plenty of time to talk.

That night, I asked her the questions I had always been afraid to ask— about Uncle Al's business, about his relationship with my father, and about the things he did and did not do. That evening was the beginning of this book.

(I think putting this recipe here is appropriate but all the other family recipes will be in the back of the book along with more family pictures.)

Meat Balls ala Capone

1 pound chuck ground once
½ pound pork ground once
½ pound veal ground once
1 tsp salt
½ tsp freshly ground black pepper
½ loaf Italian bread
small head Italian or regular parsley stems removed and blossoms chopped coarse
6 cloves garlic chopped coarse
2 eggs beaten
small jar of pine nuts
lard

Mix the 3 meats thoroughly in a large bowl.
Soak the bread in water and squeeze it until no mater remains.
Flake the bread into small pieces and add to the meat.
Add remaining ingredients.
Mix and form meatballs.
Fry in lard until brown.
Set on baking sheet in a warm (300°) oven until ready to serve.
Don't let me in the kitchen because I will eat them as soon as they come out of the oven!

2

The Promised Land

From Italy to Brooklyn, 1865 – 1922

Don't call me an Italian. I am 100 percent American.
- Al Capone

On the southwestern coast of Italy, just above the toe of the boot, lies the province of Salerno in the Campania region. Salerno is a busy port region, and it was there that the Allies landed in 1943. If you visit today, you will still find much of the ruins and destruction left by World War II.

The little town of Angri, where the parents of Al Capone were born, is nestled in the heart of Salerno at the foot of the still-active volcano, Mount Vesuvius. Just to the west, tourists flock to the ruins of Pompeii, where thousands of people were petrified in twenty feet of lava and ash when Vesuvius famously erupted in 79 A.D.

Nearly two millennia later, the town of Angri, which has survived several eruptions itself, is much quieter than neighboring Pompeii. It boasts a few ruins and is not far from coastal resorts, but it is not a tourist destination. It is a place where Italians live quietly, and have for centuries. So it was when my great-grandfather Gabriele Capone was born there to Vincenzo Capone and Maria Calabrese in 1865. My great-grandmother Teresa Raiola was born in the same town five years later, to Raffaele Raiola and Cardino Alfani. The only records of their births are their baptisms—both were baptized in San Giovanni Batista Parish, Gabriele on December 12, 1865, and Teresa on December 27, 1870.

Teresa had three older sisters who were nuns and a brother who was a priest, and so, naturally, she went into a convent when she came of age. But she realized quickly that it wasn't the life for her, and the nuns released her before she took her vows. She married Gabriele on May 25, 1891. As most marriages were in late nineteenth century Italy, theirs was an arranged marriage. At twenty-five and twenty, they were both well over the average age to marry, and I imagine their parents were relieved.

Their first son, Vincenzo, was born in Angri on March 28, 1892. At that time, Italians followed strict patterns for naming their children. The firstborn son or daughter was named for the father's parents, while the second son or daughter was named for the mother's parents. If one of the children with an important name died, the next child born of the same sex would be given his or her name. Even to this day, many Italian families still adhere to this practice. There are exceptions to the rules—but they are rare in southern Italy.

So, Vincenzo, Al Capone's oldest brother, was named for his father's father. Shortly after he was born, Gabriele moved the family to Castelammare (now called Castelammare di Stabia), not far from Salerno on the Gulf of Naples. Gabriele had trained as a barber, and he set up a shop there. To supplement the family income, Teresa baked and sold bread and took up sewing. Their second son, Raffaele or Ralph, my grandfather, was born in Castelammare two years after Vincenzo. Gabriele and Teresa eventually had nine children, but Vincenzo and Ralph were the only ones born in Italy.

By the time Ralph was born, Gabriele and Teresa had realized that life in southern Italy held little promise for them. They did not belong to the group of racketeers called the Camorra, a sort of precursor to the mafia, nor were they part of the aristocracy or church. They had little hope of advancing their station in life. And so they decided, like so many other Italians of their generation, to gamble on the American Dream.

In 1895, Gabriele entered the United States alone by way of Canada and found a job and an apartment in Brooklyn. Teresa followed shortly after with Vincenzo and Ralph in tow. They passed through Ellis Island, which automatically gave the three of them citizenship. Teresa was pregnant at the time with their third son, Salvatore or Frank, who was born in Brooklyn not long after she arrived there.

Because he had immigrated through Canada, Gabriele did not at first have citizenship papers. He took a government-run class in New York, and although he spoke no English, he passed, earning legal citizenship. My grandfather Ralph liked to tell me that his father was very proud of that accomplishment. Once he had settled the family and became a citizen, he also changed the spelling of his name to "Gabriel," and Teresa changed the spelling of hers to "Theresa." They started pronouncing their last name as

"Cap-own" rather than "Cap-own-ee." They wanted to assimilate in every way they could.

Gabriel tried opening a grocery store in Brooklyn but met with little success. He soon fell back on the training of his youth and opened a barbershop. The family was beginning to see a glimmer of possibility in their new life. On January 24, 1899, four years after they arrived in the United States, Theresa gave birth to Alphonse, who would become the famous Al Capone. He was the first of the Capone children to be conceived and born in the U.S., and my great-grandparents saw all of their hopes and dreams of becoming an American family in him.

But the family soon hit difficult times. In 1900, Theresa experienced a brutally difficult pregnancy. At the turn of the twentieth century, 90 percent of doctors were without a college education. They attended so-called "medical schools" that were condemned by the government and the press as being sub-standard. Perhaps if she had better care, the baby would have survived, but as it was, she gave birth to a stillborn son in 1900. They named him Ermino. He was followed by a baby girl in 1901, which they named Ermina in keeping with the Italian naming pattern. Ermina's brief life came to an end from meningitis in 1902.

Theresa quickly found herself pregnant with their seventh child, a sixth son born in 1903 and named Ermino. He was followed in 1906 by Alberto, in 1908 by Amedeo, and, finally, in 1912 by Mafalda. By the time I knew them, all of my uncles used nicknames. Ermino was John or "Mimi," Alberto was Bert or "Bites," and Amedeo was "Matty." Al and Ralph also each had a "mob" nickname; Al was called "Snorkey" and Ralph was "Bottles." When my father was born, they even called him "Riskey."

When the Capones settled in Brooklyn at the turn of the twentieth century, Italians were the most recent ethnic group to start immigrating en masse, making them the lowest group on the totem pole. Last to be hired and the first to be fired, people called Italian immigrants "dagos," an ethnic slur that came loosely from the Spanish name "Diego" and was a blanket term for anyone with dark hair and skin.

Gabriel and Theresa were very poor. Few apartments in New York City had indoor plumbing, and theirs, by the Navy Yard, certainly did not. They had to go down a flight of stairs into a shed in the backyard to relieve themselves and carry water up in buckets to wash themselves, the dishes, and their clothes.

The three oldest boys, Vincenzo (Jim), Ralph, and Frank, shared the same bed in the parlor, and Al slept in the bedroom with his mother and father. During the winter, they heated the apartment with a coal-fired potbelly stove in the parlor and turned the oven on in the kitchen, leaving its door open for heat. But the price of coal was very high, so they could only resort to the stove and oven heat sparingly. My grandfather Ralph would tell me stories about waking up with his eyes glued shut from ice in his lashes on bitter cold mornings.

As a barber, Gabriel was making $10 a week, considerably less than he was able to earn in Italy, and rent was as much as $4 a month. The family eventually saved enough money to move to the building on Park Avenue that also housed Gabriel's barbershop, and there, they were able to take in boarders for extra income. One of the boarders was also a barber, so he cut hair for Gabriel in lieu of paying rent, which brought in more customers and more money.

Ralph told me a story of how his parents took in a boarder who was a musician. Music fascinated Vincenzo, or Jim as he was called in America, and he asked the boarder to teach him to play his violin. Soon enough, he was much more interested in playing the violin than in going to school.

Gabriel was a stern man, and though he loved music, he ranked it second to schoolwork. He graduated from high school in Italy, a high level of education for a common person in Salerno in the nineteenth century. One of his hopes for the family was that his children would get an American education. So on the day Gabriel came home and found Jimmy playing the violin when he should have been at school, he flew into a rage. He broke the violin over his knee.

Unfortunately, Ralph and Frank never finished school; in fact, my grandfather Ralph dropped out after sixth grade. This was partly due to the fact that the family needed the extra income from his work and partly due to the fact that school was a rough place for Italian immigrants. My uncles' schoolteachers were mainly Irish, and they had no qualms about saying publicly that their "dago students" were greasy, smelly, slow learners who were not motivated to improve. None of my relatives ever had the hope of getting far enough in school to become a doctor, lawyer, or businessman. That simply was not part of the equation. They expected to be forced into finding ways to survive as best they could.

Al, however, did earn a high school diploma. Contrary to what many biographers have written, Al Capone was a high school graduate. I have a photo of Al—the earliest photo of him that I am aware of—on the day he graduated from high school, and his father is sitting proudly beside him.

———

The family continued to struggle to make ends meet. As her boys got older, Theresa would send them into the street to sell the bread she baked. The Capone boys did what they had to do to eat. They would sneak behind vendors and steal fruit off their carts to sell along with the bread. They would occasionally steal things out of stores, sell them, and use the money to buy milk to bring home to Theresa. They were typical scrappy boys growing up on the streets of Brooklyn in the early 1900s.

Over time, their troublemaking evolved into gang activity. The gangs were partly a way to survive and make a little income, and partly a way to feel a part of something in a rough community. As was portrayed in the book and film *Gangs of New York*, the gangs my grandfather and uncles ran within Brooklyn were vicious, and there were many fights. The one with the furthest-reaching consequences happened in 1908, when Jim was sixteen years old. He, Ralph, Frank, and Al all got into a big fight with some Irish boys, probably members of a rival gang. Jim pushed a boy through a glass window after he took a knife to Al's throat, then ran away scared.

When the three other boys got home and found Jim there, Al told him, "You killed that Irish kid." My uncle Jim was ashamed and afraid of what his mother and father would do. That very day, he ran away from home. The circus happened to be in New York at the time, and—just like the stuff of legend—he stole away with it.

It would be decades before the Capones ever saw or heard anything from him again. He traveled with the circus as an animal caretaker for several years, until he found a "Wild West Show" in the Midwest that seemed more interesting. He practiced his shooting skills endlessly, using milk cans and bottles as targets, until he was an expert enough marksman to become part of the show. Changing his name to Richard James Hart, after a silent movie star, he went by Jim and never revealed his Italian ancestry to anyone. As a matter of fact, most people thought he was an American Indian.

When World War I started, Jim joined the infantry, serving in France and rising to the rank of lieutenant. He even received a sharpshooter's medal from General John J. Pershing, commander of the American Expeditionary Force.

After the war ended, Jim returned to the United States, settled in Homer, Nebraska, and married in 1920. And then, his life took a truly ironic turn. He became a Prohibition agent, using clever disguises and a knack for investigation to uncover illegal bootlegging operations. He led countless raids and was the subject of local headlines throughout Nebraska. Eventually, his successes earned him the nickname "Two-Gun" Hart.

In 1926, because of his accomplishments in stemming the tide of bootlegging in Nebraska, Jim was invited to become a special agent for the Bureau of Indian Affairs. He moved to a Cheyenne Indian reservation in South Dakota, and there, during the summer of 1927, he served as the bodyguard for President Calvin Coolidge when he vacationed in the Black Hills. Just imagine—the president of the United States, protected by Al Capone's oldest brother!

And through all those years, my family knew nothing of what had become of the beloved first son. I am sure, though, that Jim kept himself informed about his famous brothers. I can imagine him reading the headlines about his outlaw family, and there he was, a celebrated law enforcer.

Meanwhile, in Chicago, the newspapers caught wind of the "missing" Capone brother. My aunt Maffie told me that on several occasions, strange men would come forward posing as Vincenzo, but Theresa always rejected them. She and Vincenzo shared a secret that no one else—including the other siblings—knew, and she wouldn't let anyone past the front door who couldn't prove he knew that long-ago story.

Vincenzo was born a frail child, and when the family immigrated to Brooklyn, he became sickly. Disease was prevalent among Italian immigrants in New York City due to their crowded quarters and limited food, so Theresa worried about him. Every day, she would take him down to the stockyards and have him drink a pint of fresh cow's blood, hoping it would strengthen him. She told him never to talk about this with anyone, not even his brothers, because they would think he was a vampire.

In 1945, Jim fell on hard times. He had no job or money, and finally, he called his mother in Chicago. Aunt Maffie, who was not even born yet when Vincent disappeared, answered the phone, and she told him to come by the house. I was there when Theresa opened the door. There was this man in his fifties, standing on the doorstep telling her in Italian that he was her long-lost son. But my grandmother didn't recognize him—the image in her mind was of her sixteen-year-old boy. She spat at him and said, "You are not my son."

Theresa walked to the parlor and sat down Jim bent down and whispered something in her ear—the secret of the cow's blood. The moment she heard it, she passed out cold. He was her son. The revelation was just as much a surprise to Jim's wife and children as well. They never knew he was a Capone. All along, they had known him as Jim Hart.

[By the way, Jim found out upon his return that he, in fact, had not killed anyone. Al had only told him he killed that young man to scare him. Do you know what Jim did when he saw Al—the legendary Al Capone, feared through all of Chicago—after all those years? He punched him in the face.]

—

When Jim ran away from home in 1908, my grandfather Ralph was suddenly thrust into the role of eldest son. In a turn-of-the-century immigrant family, this meant that he assumed responsibility for helping his parents provide for his younger brothers and sister. He was only fourteen years old but he quit school before finishing the 8th grade.

It has been written that Al Capone quite school in the 6th grade but that is not true. The only Capone sibling to quit grade school was my grandfather. All the other children were High School graduates and my Uncle Matty went to College and my Aunt Maffie to 'finishing school'.

Ralph managed to find different odd jobs here and there. He worked as a telegram messenger, a teller in a bank, and even at the Lifesaver Candy Company. Frank and Al, who were thirteen and nine when Jim disappeared, helped as much as they could by selling newspapers, but the real burden was Ralph's. Many biographers have described Ralph as either being less intelligent than Al or less of a leader, but I know that was not true. He was the businessman behind the Capone success. Al was the flamboyant face of the Outfit, but Ralph made things run from behind the scenes. He kept the books, paid out salaries, and coordinated the liquor shipments. There was a reason the Chicago Crime Commission named Ralph Public Enemy #3 behind Al's #1. Without Ralph, Al could not operate, and they knew it.

But his leadership skills didn't only apply to his life in bootlegging. He developed them and exercised them when the Capone family was under duress in those early years in Brooklyn. He learned to take care of those he loved, and this was a trait that stayed with him for all of his life. At the end of his life, when he moved out of his lodge in Wisconsin, a cousin of mine helped him pack his things. My cousin told me, "Deirdre, I found all these little pieces of paper in his strong box." They were all IOUs that people had given him, and he had never collected on. Some of them were years old. He would give this person $25, that person $500, and he didn't expect anything in return. He took care of his own.

In June 1914, as World War I erupted, my grandfather Ralph enlisted in the Navy and was sent to Paris Island. But it was quickly discovered that he had flat feet, and they sent him home. Flat feet run in the family—all the Capone men, including Al, had them. So, Ralph returned safely to Gabriel and Theresa. He would not be among the one hundred thousand Americans who died in that war.

Back in Brooklyn, he met a beautiful young Italian girl named Filomina (Florence) Muscatto in 1916. He was twenty-two, and she was only sixteen. They married, and in April 1917, their first and only child, a son, was born. That son was my father, Ralph Gabriel Capone. His arrival could not have brought more joy to my grandmother Theresa. He was the first in a new generation of Capones, and he was a boy. Women of that era saw promise in their boys—girls were expected to help with the chores.

A second boy was born in the Capone family a little more than a year later, December 4, 1918 but under less joyful circumstances. My uncle Al, then nineteen years old, was sowing his wild oats, and he got a local girl pregnant. By then, Al had already contracted syphilis, which the girl caught from him. Probably because of the disease, she had a very difficult pregnancy and died in childbirth. The boy she bore was himself weakened by the ravages of syphilis and suffered from health problems all of his life.

When my grandmother Theresa found out that Al's relationship with the girl had produced a son, she insisted that he stay with their family. He was named Albert Francis Capone, or "Sonny." Theresa wanted him to have a mother, and even though the twentieth century was well under way, arranged marriages were still perfectly common. She found a devout Irish Catholic woman, Mary (Mae) Coughlin, in her parish who was twenty one years old, nearing spinsterhood in those days. Mae was sterile due to a birth defect, and so when my grandmother pleaded with her to marry Al and raise his son as her own, she agreed. She would be a devoted mother to Sonny and wife to Al for the rest of her life.

Without warning, life for the entire Capone family turned upside-down in 1920. My great-grandfather Gabriel died suddenly of a heart attack in November at the age of fifty-five. Without him, Theresa could not keep the barbershop open. The family's means of survival was lost forever.

Although both Al and Ralph already had families of their own, they were the only ones capable of supporting their widowed mother and helping her feed her five children still at home. They needed a way to earn money—lots of money.

3

The Making of a "King"
From Brooklyn to Chicago, 1920 – 1923

I came to Chicago with forty dollars in my pocket… My son is now twelve. I am still married, and I love my wife dearly. We had to make a living. I was younger than I am now, and I thought I needed more. I didn't believe in prohibiting people from getting the things they wanted. I thought Prohibition was an unjust law, and I still do.
- Al Capone

Long before his father Gabriel died, Al Capone started developing a skill that would eventually secure him not only a fortune, but a place in history. He was becoming street wise—and he was learning how to lead a gang. It started innocently enough and I'm sure that as a teenager, Al never thought that his running with rough kids on the streets of Brooklyn would pave the way for his life's work. But slowly, over time, crime defined more and more of his life.

The Capone family needed its young sons' contributions to survive. Working six days a week at hard labor, a young man could hope to make around $900 a year in the early 1900s. But milk at that time was 33¢ a gallon. There were nine Capone mouths to feed. If the family drank only a gallon of milk a day—which is less than a glass for each person—fifteen percent of a paycheck could disappear just for milk. What about food, rent, clothing, coal, medicine…the endless list of expenses any family with young children incurs? Clearly, whatever menial labor the boys could secure wasn't enough.

Gang activity was one answer. By the time Gabriel died in 1920, Al had already been involved in crime, some petty and some not so petty, for years. It started when he was very young, simply stealing fruit and vegetables from street vendors' carts, and eventually he learned to loot trucks and warehouses. He was neither the first nor the last to resort to this solution— gangs have been in existence for as long as there have been inhabitants of this world. In fact, the word thug dates back to thirteenth century India and refers, loosely, to a member of a gang of criminals.

"We called him a 'wharf rat,'" Ralph told me in one of our talks about his boyhood with Al. "And he gradually became a fast-thinking and hard-fighting young lad." The first gang Al joined was a Brooklyn group called the James Street gang. But there were bigger fish to fry on the streets of New York City. In the early 1900s, an Italian immigrant and notorious criminal named Paolo Antonio Vaccarelli, a.k.a. Paul Kelly, formed the Italian Five Points gang. It was named for its home turf, situated in the Five Points section of Lower Manhattan, which is also called the Bowery. The gang evolved to become one of the largest and most structured street gangs in American history.

After Paul Kelly, the second in command of the Five Pointers was Johnny "the Fox" Torrio. He instituted a practice of recruiting street hoodlums into a "farm team" of young boys called the Five Pointers Juniors. At the age of twelve, Al left the James Street gang and joined the Five Pointers Juniors, where he met three other boys who would grow up to become infamous figures in American crime history: Charles "Lucky" Luciano, Meyer Lansky, and Bugsy Siegel.

Torrio, who was eighteen years older than Al, watched his new recruit with a keen interest. He saw that Al was bright and had a knack for leadership, and he began to groom him for more responsibility. When Al was still a young teenager, Torrio was confident that he had learned the ropes well, and he allowed him to graduate from being a Five Pointer Junior to a true Five Pointer.

Torrio believed in putting business first, but many other members of the Five Pointers were too accustomed to a life of petty crime and making rash, hasty decisions. Eventually, he got fed up, and with his buddy Frankie Yale, he left the Five Pointers and set up a new base of operations at the Harvard Inn in Brooklyn. Al followed them—in fact, he got the famous scar that gave rise to the nickname Scarface in a fight over a girl while working as a waiter at the Harvard Inn.

Torrio and Yale's business included extortion and a string of brothels, and they brought a network of smaller gangs under their influence. Their organization became the first mafia-style "family." Soon, they were large enough to attract the attention of corrupt politicians who saw the opportunity to control voters and elections by buying gang support—so marked the true inception of large-scale organized crime in the United States.

As Torrio's power was increasing in Brooklyn, another gang leader had made a name for himself in Chicago: James "Big Jim" Colosimo. He was an Italian immigrant who came to Chicago in the 1890s and worked as a street sweeper. He eventually involved himself in politics, worked his way up, and became a successful owner of poolrooms, saloons, and "red-light" enterprises. Eventually, he opened the famous Colosimo's Café on South Wabash Avenue.

Colosimo attained notoriety and wealth in the first decades of the twentieth century, when Italian and Sicilian immigrants were violently persecuted by the American mafia. After he opened his café, he started to receive "blackhanders," extortion letters threatening him with torture and death if he did not pay a demanded ransom. These letters were called "blackhanders" because they were signed with a drawing of a black hand. Colosimo realized he needed a smart bodyguard. In 1915, he sent for Johnny Torrio to come to Chicago.

Just after Torrio arrived, Colosimo was visited in his café by two men who told him that if he did not hand over $25,000 by the next day, he would be killed. After conferring with Torrio, Colosimo agreed to meet them the next afternoon under the railroad viaduct on Archer Avenue. When the blackhanders arrived at the appointed place, they were met by four fellows with sawed-off shotguns who killed them at pointblank range.

Torrio's method for dealing with the blackhanders was simple. He spoke to them in the only language they would understand: swift, overwhelming brute force. And they got the message. From that day on, they steered clear of Colosimo, Torrio, and, later, Al Capone.

In fact, I would learn from my grandfather Ralph that over the course of his life, many legitimate businessmen came to Uncle Al for help when they were being victimized by blackhanders. As soon as the word got out that these men were friends of Al, the extortionists would turn tail and disappear.

Colosimo was content with running his café and a few other joints, but with the advent of Prohibition in 1920, Torrio saw much broader potential. There were small-time bootleggers popping up all over Chicago, scrambling to get a foothold in this get-rich-quick business. Torrio moved quickly to shut them out and become the sole supplier of illegal alcohol in all of Cook County. He started opening "Torrio towns," the first of which was Burnham, convenient to the workers in the steel mills and oil refineries in both northwestern Indiana and South Chicago. Burnham was successful enough that Torrio eventually gained more than 100,000 employees in gambling parlors and dance halls operating day and night all over Cook County. As the automobile began to replace the horse and buggy, he started opening roadhouses along the highways. People flocked to his establishments for the slot machines, roulette, music, girls, and, of course, liquor.

In 1920, when Torrio was thirty-nine, he could no longer handle his gigantic organization alone. That's when he remembered his Five Pointer friend Al. He called my uncle and made him a proposition. At the time, he was making $100,000 a year, and he offered to pay Al $25,000, plus a 50/50 share in his bootlegging proceeds.

When Al got the call, he had a legitimate job as a bookkeeper in New Jersey. His employer liked him a lot, and when Al told him about the offer Torrio had pitched him, his boss thought it was a good deal. He gave Al $500 to enable him to make the trip. Al gave most of it to his wife Mae for rent and food. He used the rest to help defray his cost of moving to the Windy City. Years later, Al would pay back that $500—with significant interest—to show his appreciation.

When Al went to Chicago to join up with Torrio, he considered the job a trial run, and so he left Mae and Sonny in Brooklyn. But on May 11, 1920, Big Jim Colosimo was gunned down in his café, making Johnny Torrio the number one and Al, in turn, Torrio's first lieutenant.

Right on the heels of this promotion, in November 1920, Al's father died. Without warning, both he and his older brother Ralph were under tremendous financial pressure to support the family. The business, however, was starting to boom in Chicago, and so Al invited Ralph to join him in 1921. Ralph also left his wife and son behind, but both men made frequent trips back and forth to Brooklyn, bringing money to their families and to Theresa. Finally, in 1922, the brothers had saved enough money to move the entire family to Chicago.

My grandfather Ralph had a two-flat in Cicero, where there would be space for his wife and son, as well as for Theresa and all of her children. Mae and Sonny would live with Al in the apartment he rented. But Florence threw a wrench in Ralph's plan. An actress, one with a few appearances on Broadway, she refused to leave New York and her career behind.

It did not come as a particular shock to anyone in the family. When Ralph and Florence married, she was very young, and she became a mother at seventeen. She was not ready for the job—and may never have wanted it in the first place. Theresa cared for the baby, who was called Ralphie at the time, more often than Florence did.

But at first, Florence was unwilling to let Ralphie go with the rest of the Capones to Chicago, keeping him in New York with her. Theresa's heart was broken. She spent her first weeks in Chicago weeping constantly, pining for her grandson. She begged Ralph to go to New York, kidnap his own son, and bring him home.

Before Ralph had a chance to give this option any serious thought, a call came from Florence's next-door neighbor, saying that Florence had dropped off Ralphie two days before and never reappeared. That was all the invitation Ralph needed. He went immediately to New York, picked up Ralphie, and brought him to Theresa, who would raise him as a son from that day forward. The matriarch won out in the end. To her, the thought of allowing a male descendent of the Capone line—and the first-born grandson at that—grow up away from the family was inconceivable. A book was recently published claiming that the author's father was Al Capone's illegitimate son. With God as my judge, that simply could not have happened. Theresa would have died first.

Theresa was a strict Catholic. Even though she knew firsthand that Florence had no interest in being a wife and mother, she was mortified when Ralph charged Florence with desertion and filed for divorce. Divorce was simply unheard of at that time—and divorce among Catholic Italians was unthinkable. I know Theresa shamed Ralph for it, and I wonder if that had something to do with his receding into the background while Al flourished.

But although parts of the move to Chicago were painful, this was the dawning of bright years for the Capones. By 1923, only a year after the family joined him in Chicago, Al had amassed enough wealth to purchase a large house at 7244 Prairie Avenue on the South Side of Chicago. My father grew up in that house and was living there the day I was born.

Suddenly, Theresa found herself transported from the cramped, unsanitary conditions of Brooklyn to a Garden of Eden setting near Lake Michigan. She had running water, a two-flat each with its own fireplace, and a basement. Everyone in the family had their own bedroom. Not only could Theresa afford to feed her growing family and keep them healthy, she could create feasts for them in the immense kitchen. There was a backyard with an apple tree and a cherry tree and a side yard where she grew fresh tomatoes and herbs for her homemade ragu—a rich tomato sauce that everyone dubbed "Theresa's gravy." Over and over again, I heard her say that she had achieved the American dream.

But all this came at a steep price for Theresa. There were people in Chicago who wanted to kill her sons. In fact, some wanted to kill her entire family.

4.

Chicago and All That Jazz
Chicago, 1924 – 1926

The worst type is the Big Politician who gives about half his time to covering up so that no one will know he's a thief. A hard-working crook can buy these birds by the dozens, but he hates them in his heart.
- Al Capone

W. C. Fields said, "Once, during Prohibition, I had to live on nothing but food and water."

It's funny that a law passed twenty years before I was born had such an impact on my life. But if it hadn't been for the thirteen years of Prohibition from 1920 to 1933, Al Capone would not have been infamous, my family would not have been noteworthy, and I would have led a very different existence.

Prohibition was never an open and shut case, and it took not only the powerful and nationally active Temperance Movement to institute it, but also an amendment to the United States Constitution. Prohibition, which banned the sale, manufacture, and transportation of alcohol used for consumption, went into effect on January 16, 1920 by order of the Volstead Act, which Congress passed even though President Woodrow Wilson had vetoed it on October 28, 1919. The Eighteenth Amendment had to be ratified first to make the Volstead Act constitutional.

But Prohibition was extremely unpopular from its inception and quickly became vilified, especially in large cities like Chicago, when the Great Depression struck. Finally, on March 23, 1933, President Franklin Roosevelt signed into law the Cullen-Harrison Act, which nullified the Volstead Act. The Eighteenth Amendment was in turn repealed with the ratification of the Twenty-First Amendment on December 5, 1933.

Prohibition's relatively brief existence proved more than long enough to make a deep imprint on the history of this country. And as far as my family's history was concerned, those thirteen years were an epoch.

It was because of the backlash against Prohibition that the 1920s became known as the "Roaring Twenties." Speakeasies—dubbed for their bartenders' advice to patrons to "speak easy" when they ordered booze—were the birthplace of every kind of expression of freedom, from jazz music to short skirts and bobbed hair.

But, unfortunately, the Roaring Twenties didn't just roar with fun and freedom. Distributing alcohol was a big money business, where fortunes were always at stake. To a bootlegger, there was little difference between a business competitor and a blood rival. Chicago became a hotbed of violence. It is estimated that 250 gangsters were killed between 1922 and 1926, with over half of them shot by the police. Another 2,500 people died in domestic disputes, bar room fights, lovers' triangles, and robberies.

In 1924, the famous case where Leopold and Loeb kidnapped and killed their neighbor and, as would be immortalized many decades later in the stage and film musical *Chicago*, Roxie and Velma got drunk and killed their boyfriends. Chicago's homicide rate was 24 percent higher than the national average—while New York City's was 31 percent below the national average.

In 1924, the *Chicago Tribune* began printing a clock face in its weekly edition. The clock had three hands called the "Hands of Death." The first was labeled "Moonshine," the second "Guns," and the third "Autos." Drunk driving had made its debut.

The Capone family was far from immune to the death toll. In 1923, Johnny Torrio and Al moved the operation of their gang, which they were now calling the Chicago Outfit, from Chicago to the western suburb of Cicero. Even their deep pockets had no influence on Chicago's reform mayor, William Dever, and so they figured Cicero would be better for business.

At that time, my uncle Frank joined Al and Ralph in running the Outfit. Al did not yet have the stature he would gain in the following years, and so it was at first the charismatic Frank who served as the Outfit's front man. But Frank's charisma had a flip side. Al was famously prone to violence, but my grandfather Ralph told me that Frank was infinitely worse. Johnny Torrio had taught Al to cool off and negotiate, and Al took that training well. Frank, on the other hand, saw no cause for talk. If someone crossed him, he reacted instantly—and crazily. Ralph quoted Frank as saying, "You never get no back-talk from a corpse."

Frank was, in Ralph's opinion, the best looking of all the brothers. He was tall and lean with thick, dark hair. Unfortunately, I was born many years after his violent death, and so I never saw him personally. The only photo of him I know of is the one that was taken at the morgue. In it, he bears a frightening resemblance to my dad.

When the Outfit moved to Cicero, Frank took on the task of dealing with the town council. He had perfected the appearance of a successful businessman and always dressed in well-tailored suits. He would first approach candidates for office and get them to promise to allow the Outfit to operate their illegal gambling dens and brothels without interference from the police. Once they agreed to play ball, he would make sure they won come Election Day.

But Frank was not always even-keeled enough to think through his actions carefully. Ralph told me a story about how a Capone-endorsed candidate started complaining that he was not making as much money as some of the lower-ranked guys in the Outfit. He demanded a percentage of the Outfit's income. Al was more than nettled, and he said to Frank, "Why the hell did you choose such a stupid candidate?"

Frank's violent tendencies ultimately cornered him. When the Cicero city manager, Joseph Z. Klenha, was up for re-election in the 1924 primary, the Outfit positioned themselves outside the voting locations with sawed-off shotguns and Tommy guns. They asked each voter who they were going to vote for, and if the answer wasn't, "Klenha," they made sure that voter left the premises without casting a ballot. But Frank decided to take things a step further, just for good measure. It was reported that he ransacked Klenha's opponent's office, injuring several campaign employees.

When reports of election fraud reached the Cook County judge, Edmund J. Jareki, he deputized about seventy Chicago policemen and sent them to Cicero to restore order. The group of policemen that went to the polling place near the Western Electric Company in Cicero dressed in plain clothes and arrived in large black touring sedans like those used by the Outfit and its rival gangs.

This was the polling place where Frank, Al, and several other men were soliciting votes with their guns. When they saw men show up in plain clothes, they hesitated for a moment, thinking they might have members of the North Side Mob on their hands. But they quickly realized that the men were in fact police officers, and they ran into the street in different directions. My uncle Frank was shot in the back in the middle of the street. My grandfather Ralph swore that, contrary to the police reports, Frank never drew his weapon on the officers.

Now here is the part of the story that has never been told before. According to my grandfather, Frank was very involved with a girl who had been dating a Chicago police captain. She fell in love with Frank and broke things off with the cop—who then made it known that he was out to kill Frank. I think he ultimately did.

Ralph told me about how he warned Frank that his relationship with the girl was risky, but Frank waved him off. He was sure the Outfit's boys would protect him, and for laughs, he goaded the cop. He would buy the girl expensive, flashy jewelry, and take her out to all the right places where he knew they would be seen. My grandfather believed—and I believe him—that Frank tragically underestimated that police captain.

Frank was dead, and my grandmother Theresa's life was shattered. She was a superstitious woman, and she believed deeply that a curse had been placed on her boys. After Uncle Frank's funeral, she asked Uncle Al to send her back to Italy. She went back to Angri, to the convent where her sisters lived, where she prayed for forgiveness for more than half a year. My aunt Mae took care of my father, who was seven years old, and Sonny in her absence. Theresa returned to Chicago in November of 1924.

By 1926, the Outfit's activities had gotten so hot that most of the members began sending their children to boarding school. Aunt Maffie and Uncle Matty, both still teenagers, were sent away, along with Sonny and my father, who were eight and nine years old respectively.

My father had been living with his "mamacita" Theresa at the Prairie Avenue house, while his father Ralph lived in his own apartment. Al, on the other hand, lived with Mae and Sonny on the second floor. Although Al was seldom home, my father noticed that Ralph interacted with him far less than Al interacted with Sonny, and he resented him for it. I'm not sure that my father was sorry to go when he was sent to St. John's Prep School in St. Cloud, Minnesota. He liked school and excelled at it, and he also loved to act in school plays—a talent he probably inherited from his mother.

I do know, however, that my grandfather was furious that his family had been threatened. There was an unspoken code that families were off limits. As Ralph put it many years later, "Those stupid assholes didn't play by the rules."

Though the Outfit's operations were always dangerous, 1926 marked the start of wild, unpredictable times. Uncle Al had the house on Prairie Avenue fortified, installing iron bars on the basement windows. Theresa shut all the drapes that hung on the first floor windows and never opened them again. I can still remember how dark the first floor was and how bright and sunny the upstairs was. And in addition to fortifying the family home, the brothers fortified themselves. They wore body armor and hired bodyguards who constantly shadowed them and became fixtures at the Prairie Avenue house doors.

But Al and Ralph weren't running risks for free. The U. S. Attorney's Office in Chicago estimated that the Outfit grossed over $105 million in 1926. You'd have to multiply that amount by at least ten to find its worth in today's dollars. The money came from hundreds of bars in Cicero and, later, thousands in Chicago, almost every one of them operated without fear of reprisal from politicians, judges, or policemen, many of whom were on Al's payroll. Moreover, the populace was on the Outfit's side. Law-abiding Chicagoans thought nothing of walking into an illegal bar and ordering a beer. Al was providing people with what they wanted—booze, booze, and more booze. (For the record, my grandfather ran all this without the use of a fax machine or a cell phone.)

The family enjoyed the fruits of its labor immensely. My father, Sonny, and their friends got to ride to the movies in a black touring sedan with an armed driver, each carrying a hundred-dollar bill in his pocket. They had the best seats at every major event that came through the city, like the circus or touring stage shows. They had front row seats at both Cubs and White Sox games.

I have never come across a historical account of those years that mentions how Al and Ralph handled the stress of operating a high-yield business in the face of constant threats to their lives. I know, however, from my own experience of them that they did take time to relax.

Ralph told me stories of visiting Hot Springs, Arkansas, with Al for rest and relaxation. The resorts there were classified as a safe haven, no matter whose side you were on. Ralph talked about how it was entirely possible to find himself sitting in a hot bath with the FBI director. This was also the place where he and Al could meet with the leaders of rival gangs and share information—anything from where to buy the best goods at the best prices to where to find girls for a short holiday.

Obviously, in Al and Ralph's line of work, beautiful women were not hard to come by. With all the money and influence they had, and all the time they spent away from home, they were bound to attract admirers—and they didn't do much to discourage them. My uncle Bites dated a woman named Loraine, whom everyone called Larry. She told me that during that period, the woman Ralph was seeing, and later married, Valma Pheasant, said to her, "Better spend their money first because they'll just piss it away, anyway!"

Gossip columns about Al and Ralph's exploits with women—complete with photographic evidence—started appearing in the papers. And, of course, my father, Sonny, and Aunt Mae saw those articles. It was not easy for them to take. There were murmurings in the family about how Aunt Mae once said to Sonny, "Your father broke my heart, please don't you break it also."

Al's penchant for pleasure wasn't limited to women, though. He was a connoisseur of good music, and the height of his wealth happily coincided with the explosion of jazz music on the American cultural scene. Chicago was the center of the jazz craze, and both Al and Ralph were the biggest jazz impresarios in the city. All the best jazz musicians wanted to play their clubs.

When Louis Armstrong was playing with his wife Lil Hardin's band at the Dreamland Café in 1925, my grandfather Ralph heard him perform. They got to talking, and Louis told him about the famous Cotton Club in Harlem and how it provided opportunities for black musicians. That club, incidentally, was owned and run by Owney Madden, a prominent bootlegger and gangster. Louis's stories planted a seed in Ralph's mind, and pretty soon, he was running one of the grandest nightclubs of the day in Cicero, a little joint he called the *Cotton Club*.

It was there that he and Al gave black musicians like Earl "Fatha" Hines, Duke Ellington, Cab Calloway, Jellyroll Morton, and Fats Waller their professional starts. Very few people know that it was my grandfather Ralph who "discovered" Ethel Waters. Ralph once took me to night club named *The Chez Paree* in Chicago to see Nat King Cole sing and play the piano. After his set, he came over to our table, and right away, I could see that he and my grandfather knew each other well. He invited us to come backstage to show us around.

When I asked Ralph how he knew Nat King Cole, he said, "Oh, he used to play in our nightclubs when he was still in high school. He wasn't known for his singing in those days, but man could he play piano. We got along OK, but he really loved Al."

Life was difficult and dangerous for black musicians in Chicago in the 20s. Many club owners were known to extort money from their black performers, but Al protected the entertainers who worked for him. He even supplied some with bodyguards when it was necessary.

As Ralph explained to me, "Al really liked the blacks; he appreciated their music more than I did. To me it was just a business. As long as they showed up, kept their noses clean, and the customers liked them, they had no problem with me. But if they screwed up, they were out on their ass. Al was more lenient, so we had some arguments about who was gonna stay and who was gonna go. Usually Al won. Sometimes Al would throw a private party and Fats or the King would play all night, and after every couple songs, Al would stuff a hundred dollar bill in his pocket.

Al would tell me 'Ralph, these poor bastards are going through the same kind of crap that us Italians had to put up with a generation ago. Even worse! So I'm glad to help them make a living, especially when they are as talented as these guys are.'"

In a 1931 article in *Harpers Monthly*, Katherine Fullerton Gerould called Al Capone "one of the central figures of our time." In a way, he represented a way of life. Of course, part of his legendary stature involves the mystique of crime, but he also stands out as a figure who championed central elements of American culture when they were first emerging in the 20s, most notably jazz, and the freedom and individuality that went along with it.

As Gerould puts it, "Capone was a Ford or a Rockefeller with a shoulder holster. He flatly broke laws his public either wanted broken or cared little about, yet hadn't the nerve or resources to break themselves, and he might personally knock an officious lawmaker down the stairs. He killed or had killed only those that the public, had they dared, would have happily dispatched of themselves.

It is not because Capone is different that he takes the imagination: it is because he is so gorgeously and typically American."

5

Trading the Chicago Outfit for the Chicago Cubs

Chicago, 1926 – 1929

Let the worthy citizens of Chicago get their liquor the best way they can.
I'm sick of the job. It's a thankless one and full of grief.
- Al Capone

As the 20s drew to a close, Al began to see the writing on the wall. Prohibition was probably the most despised law ever enacted in the United States, and the most ignored. By 1930, there were more than 10,000 illegal drinking establishments in Chicago alone. All of the largest and most prominent of these—and the majority of the smaller ones, too—were controlled by Uncle Al. He was generating more than $100 million a year in income, all of it in cash.

But he could sense the impending end of Prohibition, so he actively looked for ways to get into another business—a legitimate business. Like Michael Corleone in *The Godfather*, Al desperately wanted to funnel his cash into building a more secure life for himself and his family.

My grandfather Ralph told me about the emotional toll Al's dangerous lifestyle was taking on him. To both Al and Ralph, there were two sacred rules for living. First, family is everything. And second, your word is your bond. So when they started to see the viciousness that was proliferating among the Chicago gangs, and the willingness many gangsters had to backstab, renege on their word, and even threaten the families of other gangsters, they wanted out.

And in addition to fearing for his family, Al feared for his own life. His wife, Aunt Mae, once told me, "I don't know if you knew this, Deirdre, but your uncle Al had bad dreams almost every night. He would wake up and the bed sheets would be soaked with sweat. I'd have to change the sheets in the middle of the night.

One recurring nightmare was about the time in 1926 when he was having lunch with Frankie Rio at the Hawthorne Inn and seven cars pulled up and fired thousands of machine gun bullets into the restaurant. When it actually happened, he came out without a scratch, but in his dream he was riddled with bullets. He was burning with pain and bleeding all over."

Mae believed that Al had a gift of prophecy, and that his dreams foretold events before they happened. To her, and to Al too, that was how he managed to escape the many dangers that perpetually dogged him. But there was one recurring dream that both he and Mae hated, and that Al couldn't shake. In this dream, he watched the police pull bodies from the Chicago River—the bodies of Mae and Sonny. He was terrified this dream would come true, and it was one of the reasons he bought a house in Florida—so that Mae and Sonny could live away from Chicago. It was also a major reason he was so eager to find a way out of the Outfit.

Ralph remembered Al going on long rants about the madness of running the Outfit. He could quote these rants from memory: "I've got to get out, Ralph. I've got enough money. I don't need this insanity. Weiss, Moran, and those other assholes are idiots. [Hymie Weiss and Bugsy Moran were members of the Outfit's rival gang, the North Side gang] You can't do business with crazy people. I've been shot at, almost poisoned with prussic acid, and there is an offer of $50,000 to any gunman who can kill me. They don't understand that there's enough for all of us. They don't have to cut in on my territory. What do they expect me to do, let them get away with it? They agree to something, then they break the deal. They're pissed because I run a better business. I make more money than they do. They are jealous bastards. They want what I have. You can't trust 'em. Their word doesn't mean shit. I run my outfit like a business. It is a business."

Al would often follow these rants by drifting into a list of his big ideas for leaving the Outfit. He had a number of different plans for what he could do with his life in the legitimate world. One idea was to get one of his writer friends, like Ben Hecht (who would write the screenplay for Gone with the Wind in 1939) or Damon Runyon (who wrote the musical Guys and Dolls), to help him write his autobiography.

Runyon was a particularly close buddy to both Al and Ralph. He loved Theresa's cooking and was often a guest at the Prairie Avenue home when he visited Chicago. Many of his stories and characters are based on his relationship with my uncle and grandfather. Al hoped that if Runyon helped him write a decent book, it could be made into a movie, in which he would play himself. He said he wouldn't have to be a great actor—he'd just be himself. And he would invite performers like Louis Armstrong and Duke Ellington to play in scenes shot at the Cotton Club.

Runyon and Hecht both shared interest in the idea. But when Al approached them about the project, neither could find time within their schedules. Barely a few years later, he was convicted of income tax evasion and sent to prison—and so the book never happened.

Another idea Al bandied around was to release a line of designer clothing. In Chicago in the 20s, Al was a fashion plate. He dressed impeccably in custom tailored suits, coats, hats, shirts, and ties—and he always chose the finest, imported materials. Men all over Chicago copied his "look," and so eventually a well-known clothing designer approached Al about creating the "Al Capone Collection."

At first, Al kind of liked the idea. Clothing is certainly a "legit" business, and he thought he could make enough money with the line to get out of the rackets completely. But he was also concerned that getting into fashion would detract from his tough image. He understood that no matter how much he distanced himself from the Outfit, he might always be under threat—and so becoming a fashion icon didn't seem like the safest new identity to take on.

Al turned his keen businessman's eye to less conspicuous businesses—and happened upon the dairy industry. As he put it himself, "You gotta have a product that everybody needs every day. We don't have it in booze. Except for the lushes, most people only buy a couple of fifths of gin or Scotch when they're having a party. The working man laps up half a dozen bottles of beer on Saturday night, and that's it for the week.

But with milk! Every family, every day, wants it on the table. The people on Lake Shore Drive want thick cream in their coffee. The big families out back of the yards have to buy a couple of gallons of fresh milk every day for the kids. Do you guys know there's a bigger markup in fresh milk than there is in alcohol? Honest to God, we've been in the wrong racket right along."

Al and Ralph already had access to bottling facilities for their bootlegging business, so it wasn't hard for them to add milk to their slate of products. My grandfather Ralph is credited with being the first to date-stamp milk bottles. Though most people think he got his nickname "Bottles" from being a bootlegger, it actually came from his clever idea about putting the date on milk bottles so that people at the grocery store would know how fresh the product was.

But selling milk and other soft beverages never quite took off in the same way selling liquor had. And Al wasn't ready to trade in his high-rolling lifestyle for the more tame life of a milkman. He enjoyed being a big shot and courting the limelight—so much so that he often went so far as to hold press conferences. What other big time racketeer had both the panache—and the courage—to do that?

Al understood that his celebrity status put him in a unique position to help people. He didn't want to lose that leverage. Not only was he committed to the performers and musicians who worked for him, he also wanted to have the social clout needed to step in where others—even law enforcement—often fell short. For example, he volunteered all of his resources to aid in the search for the kidnapped Lindberg baby.

"A kidnapper is no better than a rat," Al said, "and I don't approve of his racket because it makes the kidnapped man's wife and kiddies worry so much. I shall be glad to help Chicago in this emergency." The police, unfortunately, did not take him up on his offer. Maybe the outcome would have been different if they had.

So, Al kept searching for ways to quit the Outfit without completely relinquishing his position of power. He eventually stumbled on the idea of purchasing the Edgewater Beach Hotel, north of the loop on the shore of Lake Michigan. He thought it was the classiest hotel in Chicago, and he was going to make the penthouse suite his summer residence. Then he would redesign the hotel nightclub and book all his favorite entertainers.

Edgewater Beach Hotel c.1920

As Ralph recalled, "He was really enthused about that idea. He kept pacing back and forth, puffing on his cigar while telling me about it."

But Al's schemes got grander still. His biggest idea was to buy the Chicago Cubs, Wrigley Field and all.

When he pitched the idea to his brother, Ralph said, "You must be crazy. The commissioner of baseball would never approve the sale to you with your background."

But Al had already thought of that. He had decided he wouldn't be the owner of record—instead, he'd ask a friend in sports to front for him. He felt pretty confident that he could convince his pal Jack Dempsey, or maybe Gabby Hartnett. If not, there were always his friends in show business—he and Ralph discussed putting the idea to Al Jolson, George Jessel, or Harry Richman.

But at that time, my grandfather Ralph still needed convincing. He told me about the back and forth he and Al went through over the idea.

"Why the Cubs?" Ralph wanted to know. "Why not the White Sox?"

"For lots of reasons!" was Al's response. "For one thing, I love Wrigley Field. It's my favorite ballpark. Besides, I've been associated with the South Side too much. Chicago's my town, and that includes the North Side, which I think will one day become bigger than the South Side.

Anyway, Wrigley doesn't know baseball," Al continued. "He knows gum." This was, at the heart of it, his most important reason for wanting to buy the Cubs. He loved baseball. All the Capone boys did. Baseball was America's favorite pastime, and these boys were Americans, through and through.

"I could run the organization better than Wrigley can," Al boasted. "If I don't take it off his hands, he'll run that team into the ground before long."

Al did know baseball well. And he already had a number of ideas for making the Cubs the next great American team. He had devised a plan to trade for Babe Ruth by paying Yankees owner Colonel Jacob Ruppert—who wasn't really a colonel but was a former brewer—$500,000 in cash. According to Al, he had already talked to the Babe about using him as both a player and manager. The Babe was very excited about the idea; he had always wanted to be a manager, but Colonel Rupert wouldn't give him the chance.

Al had also talked with Gus Greenlee, a bootlegger friend of his who owned the negro team, the Crawfords, about buying the contracts of Satchel Paige and another of his stars. They would have been the first blacks to play in the major leagues. Ralph told Al he was crazy, but once Al made up his mind to do something, there was no talking him out of it.

Ralph's biggest question, though, was still unanswered. "What if Wrigley doesn't want to sell?"

"Don't worry, he'll sell."

"How do you know?"

"Because I've got something on the Wrigleys. Shit, I've got something on all the big shots in Chicago. Everyone, even the fine upstanding citizens, the pillars of the community—especially them—has something to hide. Something they don't want the public, the law, or their wives to know. Don't worry—he'll sell!"

"So you'll rat on him if he doesn't?" Ralph pressed.

"No, I wouldn't do that. I won't have to! We just let him know that we know, and he'll listen to reason. Of course, I'll pay him a fair price. I'll give him the going rate for a major league team. Maybe even better than the going rate. I'm not hard to do business with."

"What would you offer him for it?" Ralph finally asked.

And then, as he told me the story, Ralph broke into a big grin. "I swear, Deirdre," he said. "Al said to me, 'I'll make him an offer he can't refuse.'"

Ralph let out a low laugh. "When I heard that line used in *The Godfather*, I nearly fell out of my seat. The same words Al used forty years before! Just a coincidence, I guess, but it made me laugh."

He sighed and shook his head. "Deirdre," he said, "when Al first told me about his plans for the Cubs and the Babe, I was very skeptical, especially about bringing black players into major league baseball. But the more I thought about it, the more I began to believe he could pull it off. He had a great imagination, tons of money, a lotta balls, and he had a way of making things happen. What would have been a pipe dream for me or anybody else was a real possibility for Al, my kid brother. They broke the mold when he was born. If he could have pulled this off, he would have changed the history of baseball, big time."

6

The Saint Valentine's Day Truth
Chicago, February 14, 1929

They've hung everything on me but the Chicago fire.
- Al Capone

In 1958, with my world turned upside-down, I turned—as I always did—to the Capones. As it turned out, my own heartache became a path into the heart of my family which I had been trying to understand since my father's death.

When I went to my aunt Maffie for advice, she suggested I go to Wisconsin to spend some time with my grandfather at his lodge.

"Do you really think he'd want me up there?" I asked. My grandfather had built the lodge as a sort of man's retreat. It was where he and Al often went to escape the business of Chicago, and though I had loved my summers there as a little girl, I didn't want to intrude on Ralph's solitude.

But Aunt Maffie responded with one loud, "Ha!"

"Are you kidding?" She asked me. "He adores you. He'd love to have you visit."

She called him up right in that moment, and by the next morning, I was on a bus to one of my favorite places in the world, the lodge in Mercer, Wisconsin.

So many good childhood memories ran through my head as the bus pulled out of Chicago—the fresh air, the starry nights, the winter-time rides in a reindeer-pulled sleigh, fishing and swimming in the lake in the summer, and being with my dad. I felt a tear roll down my cheek, but wiped it away quickly, saying to myself, "Snap out of it, Deirdre. You can't bring him back, but he lives in your heart. And you'll feel closer to him at the lodge."

I could hardly wait to get there and be with my grandfather. I not only wanted to see him, I wanted to ask him a lot of questions. I had already embarked on my project of unearthing all the information I could about my family, and I kept running up against a persistent question, the darkest of the blots on the Capone name: the Saint Valentine's Day Massacre. I knew that if anyone could help me understand how my uncle Al could possibly have been involved in such a senseless crime, it would be my grandfather Ralph.

Late one night at Recap Lodge I sat with my grandfather in his kitchen. He ate a salami sandwich, had a couple of drinks, and I guessed that meant he would be more willing than usual to talk about the old days.

Without my prompting, he suddenly murmured that he was sorry he had not been a better father to my father, and that I had born the consequences of it after my dad's suicide. He told me that since his son didn't have a mother, he thought it would be better for him to let his grandmother Theresa raise him. And he also thought it would be safer.

"Al and I had to work hard all the time not to get ourselves killed," Ralph said, "we had a business to run, and the whole family—including your dad—depended on the money from that business. There were many people who were trying to take our business away from us, and there were many people who wanted to see us dead."

I took a deep breath. "Ralph," I said—he insisted that I call him Ralph and not grandpa—"was that what happened at the Saint Valentine's Day Massacre? Was Al trying to protect the family?"

The story I knew was this: The St. Valentine's Day Massacre happened on the morning of February 14, 1929. Seven men sat in a garage at 2122 N. Clark Street waiting for George "Bugs" Moran, chief of the North Side gang. They also waited for a delivery of booze "hijacked off a boat," and, later that afternoon, they all planned to go to Detroit to pick up some whisky.

Ralph shook his head pointedly. "Al did not plan it," he said firmly. "In fact, that's the last thing he would have wanted. He was furious when he heard about it. He phoned me and was really steaming. He said, 'That crazy bastard McGurn! What's he trying to do, crucify me?'" Al was in Florida at the time of the Saint Valentine's Day Massacre and left one of his partners, Jack "machine gun" McGurn, in charge.

Ralph explained to me that before he left, Al had been particularly worried about the activities of a rival bootlegger and head of the North Side gang, Bugs Moran. McGurn had told Al he could handle Moran.

"OK, then handle him," Al had said. "Put the fear of God in him. Run him out of town…whatever. Just do it in a way that won't bring us a lot of heat. I've got enough problems as it is."

And McGurn came back with, "Nothing to worry, boss. Leave it to me. I'll take care of him."

Then, after the massacre hit the papers, Al exploded to Ralph over the phone. "So what does the asshole do?" He ranted. "He mows down seven people at once! This kind of thing can ruin us. The *Tribune* and the rest of the press will never get off this. Sure as hell they're already blaming me for it, even though I'm over a thousand miles away in Florida. And the guys back east aren't gonna be happy about this either. They'll never believe I didn't plan the whole fuckin' mess. And to top it off, he didn't even get Moran. That son of a bitch is still walkin' around Chicago. Ralph, this a fuckin' nightmare. Wake me up, will ya?"

It seemed to me that Al was clearly not directly involved, but hearing about this rant from Ralph still didn't clear him entirely in my mind. If McGurn was responsible and McGurn worked for Al…it would be tough to say that Al was innocent. So far, Ralph hadn't yet told me anything that contradicted the account I'd already read in countless newspaper clippings and that was popularly accepted as immutable fact.

The men were Pete Gusenberg and his brother Frank, who were both payroll robbers; James Clark, a stickup man; Johnny May, a safe-blower as well as the Moran gang's auto mechanic; Al Weinshank, a speakeasy operator; Adam Heyer, the owner of the garage; Dr. Reinhardt Schwimmer, an optometrist. Oh, and a German shepherd was chained to one of the trucks in the garage.

The garage door opened, and two men dressed as policemen entered the garage followed by three other men. The intruders lined all seven occupants up against the wall and machine-gunned them down instantly. Only the dog was left unharmed.

An inquiry by police and the state's attorney identified three of the five men: Fred Burke, Jack McGurn, and John Scalise. Gus Winkler was one of the men not identified.

Although this description of what happened on that gruesome Valentine's Day is the commonly accepted version offered in books and movies, my grandfather told me an entirely different story that evening in Wisconsin. His version of the story has never been printed anywhere before.

This is what he told me.

"Deirdre, the day after I talked with Al, I confronted McGurn and told him how pissed Al was with him. You know what he said? He said, 'God damn it, Ralph, I swear I didn't do it. Hell, if I'd had done it I would have done it right. Gimme some credit. I'm a professional. I know Moran like I know the back of my hand. If he wasn't there do you think I would have mowed down those other assholes? Shit, they weren't even his key men.

Let me tell you what I think happened. In fact, I'm sure it went down this way. The day before Valentine's Day, I was parked on Clark Street a few doors down and across the street from Moran's garage. I had been doing that and watching the Parkway Hotel where Moran lives for about a week. Your kid brother Matty was with me most of the time. I was trying to establish a pattern of behavior so I could take him down, *like that.*' McGurn snapped his fingers. 'No muss, no fuss, no loose ends. You know I've been getting smarter in my old age.

Anyway on the thirteenth, Matty and I notice a car—a caddy—full of cops, driving slowly past the garage headed south. Then a couple of minutes later it comes back in the other direction. This time, I caught a glimpse of the driver and he looked familiar. I don't mind tellin' ya, I was getting nervous. I'm thinkin', did they recognize me? Do they have another warrant for my arrest?

When they drove by the third time, I said, *That's it, Matty, we're gettin' the hell out of here.* I swear to God that's the last time I was near that garage. If you don't believe me, ask Matty.

'Listen Ralph,' McGurn went on. 'Here's the way I got it figured. Those cops were out to get Moran. I heard rumors that some cops were hijackin' his booze and Moran was gonna rat them out to his captain friends on the force. I can't prove it, but I think those cops did the shooting. Hell, they probably thought Moran was one of the guys they blasted, the assholes.'"

My grandfather poured himself another scotch, lit a cigar, and took a big puff. "Deirdre," he said, "I checked with your Uncle Matty, and he backed up what McGurn told me. But it didn't really make any difference. The newspapers and just about everyone was blaming Al for it."

As you can imagine, I wanted to believe my grandfather Ralph more than anything. But I took my time. I had no corroboration of my grandfather's account of the Saint Valentines Day Massacre until about six years later when Uncle Matty had dinner with Bob and me at our house shortly after we married. After we'd had dinner and the kids were put to bed, we sat down and relaxed in the living room with a drink. Matty smoked a cigar that really stunk, but, in those days, we tolerated smoking in the house.

We were chatting away about the Cubs, the Bears, and boxing—Matty's favorite sport—when I suddenly remembered what Ralph said about Matty being in the car with McGurn the day before the massacre. I asked him about it.

At first his eyebrows shot up in surprise. "Who told you about that?" He asked.

I told him how I had gone to visit my grandfather and spent a lot of time talking with him about the years before I was born.

"Wow, you must have caught him in a weak moment," Matty said. "He hardly ever talked about shit like that." In those days, I never used profanity. My grandmother Theresa taught me that bad language is not something a lady stoops to. But I sure heard plenty of it from her sons, so it didn't faze me to hear Matty use it in my house, as long as my kids weren't listening.

Matty went on to confirm everything my grandfather had told me—except that he added that he and McGurn were in <u>his</u> car on February 13, and <u>he</u> was driving.

Matty was never heavily involved in the Outfit. He was weaker than and not as bright as Uncle Al and Ralph, but he liked being known as a Capone and a big shot, so he kind of bragged about working side-by-side with McGurn.

Suddenly, Bob spoke up. "This reminds me of something my dad told me about what my uncle Tommy said about Valentine's Day, 1929," Bob said. Tommy May's brother was one of the seven men killed that day: John May. John always insisted that he was just an auto mechanic for Moran and not a criminal. All the same, he had access to information, because he had been complaining just prior to the shooting that some crooked cops were hijacking Bugs Moran's booze, and Moran was going to put a stop to it and get them kicked off the force. Based on those complaints, Tommy had told Bob's dad on two or three occasions that he was sure it was cops and not Capone who did it.

At that point, I was pretty sure I had the truth about the Saint Valentines Day Massacre. I heard pretty much the same story coming not only from the family of Al Capone, but also the family of one of the victims. And I had read in clippings from the Chicago newspapers that one of the seven slaughtered men, Frank Gusenberg, survived long enough to tell police

Sergeant Thomas Loftus, "Cops did it." Now, from what I heard about Frank Gusenberg, he had enough interaction with the police to know a cop when he saw one.

But still, this account was one I never read in any book about Uncle Al and never saw in any movie or television show about him. I started to believe the massacre was an example of what Al was talking about when he said, "I've done a lot of bad things, things I wish I didn't have to do to survive, but I haven't done half of the rotten things that they say I've done."

After Matty left our house that night I told myself, "OK, maybe I'm easily convinced because I'm a Capone and would like to think that my family didn't kill those seven men." I heard my family's story and Bob's story, but I knew that others could and would say these were biased accounts. And as much as I wanted to believe Ralph and Matty, I couldn't deny they had a vested interest in clearing their brother's name. I needed more verification—something that came from outside the Capone sphere of influence.

Just recently, I got that verification. A historian, David Ward, published an excellent and well-documented book called *Alcatraz-The Gangster Years*. It includes a section about the slaughter on N. Clark Street. In it, Ward disclosed an announcement made by Frederick D. Silloway, the local prohibition administrator, shortly after the massacre. He was quoted in the newspapers as saying, "The murderers were not gangsters. They were Chicago policemen. I believe the killing was the aftermath to the hijacking of 500 cases of whiskey belonging to the Moran gang by five policemen six weeks ago...I expect to have the names of these five policemen in a short time. It is my theory that in trying to recover the liquor, the Moran gang threatened to expose the policemen and the massacre was to prevent the exposure."

When I read the newspaper accounts of the Saint Valentine's Day Massacre, I knew in my bones that they were not true. My uncle Al Capone was not a monster.

In the recently published book, *Get Capone* by Jonathan Eig, the same evidence was uncovered.

It took me about fifty years to fully convince myself that at least this one event—a shocking, unforgettable event to be sure—was not, regardless of what I may have read or heard, ordered by Uncle Al. By publishing the evidence I've gathered, maybe I can divest my subconscious of some of the guilt I've carried merely because I was born a Capone.

There is another chapter in the story of the Saint Valentine's Day Massacre. During the time I spent with my grandfather in 1958, he—after much pressing—finally told me a little more about three men in Al's gang who died mysteriously. I learned from Ralph that these men were double-crossing Al by working for both him and Bugs Moran at the same time. They were probably the ones who saved Bugs Moran's life by telling him that the cops were out to kill him and that he shouldn't go to the garage on the morning of February 14.

The facts on record, which I knew long before asking for Ralph's account, were these: Early on in the gang wars, in 1924, John Scalise and Albert Anselmi were accused of killing a man named Dion O'Banion. My uncle Al paid for their defense, and they got off. On May 8, 1929, the bodies of Scalise, Anselmi, and another man who worked for Al named John Gunita were found in a ditch in Indiana. They had been beaten on the head by blunt objects reported as baseball bats and shot. This became known as the "Baseball Bat Incident."

This was a subject that my grandfather really didn't want to talk about. I kept pressing him, and he finally said, "Look, Deirdre, all I can tell you about that incident is that Al got a couple of tips from very reliable sources that those three guys, Anselmi, Scalise, and Gunita, who he had been a friend to many times, had planned to kill him so they could take over the Outfit. There was a man named Joe Aiello, an associate of Bugs Moran, who wanted to cut in on the alcohol rackets. He made an offer of $50,000 to anyone who 'bumps off Capone.'

To get that fifty grand, Anselmi, Scalise, and Gunita decided to use their high status in the Outfit to kill Al and then work with Aiello to take over Chicago. They offered Al's chef, Peppe, $5,000 to poison Al. Peppe told Al about the threat and kept the money."

Ralph went on, "It was also reported that it was them that warned Bugs that the cops were out to get him and not to go to the garage that morning. They were clearly on Bugs's payroll and only pretending to be loyal to Al. They were double-crossers.

One of the reports said that they thought they had better take me out as well as the other brothers at the same time to avoid retaliation. So they were going to blow up the house on Prairie Avenue on a Sunday when we were all there having dinner. They felt they could pull it off because they were insiders and the bodyguards wouldn't suspect them. Deirdre, if they had pulled it off, Grandma Capone, Aunt Maffie, your father...all of us would have been killed.

When Al heard this, he went berserk. I have never seen him that mad. He was like a wild man. But a little while later, he suddenly calmed down. After a few minutes of silence he began to smile. I said, 'What are you thinking about?' He just lit up a cigar, grinned, and said, 'I think it's time to throw a party for our friends.'

That's all I'm going to say about this," Ralph said, looking at me sternly. "There had always been a code of honor that Al and most of the other guys in the business lived by. And that was that no matter how pissed off you were at your enemies, the innocent members of their families were off limits. And nobody loved his family more than my brother Al. And you never double-cross your friends. Too bad some guys didn't live by that code. If you ask me, those guys got what they deserved."

I cannot pretend that my grandfather Ralph and my uncle Al had stainless hands. I cannot make them out to be heroes. But I am a Capone. Their blood runs through my veins. And I knew them. I heard the deep rumble of their voices; I felt their big arms around me; I smelled their skin.

———

That stay in Mercer and those conversations with my grandfather got me through a very tough time in my life. But what helped me even more than feeling close to my grandfather was feeling close to my father again— as I knew I would at the lodge. I had so many childhood memories of happy times with my father in Mercer, and being there again made me feel closer to him than I had ever felt since the day he took his life. To this day, I am encouraged by the feeling that his spirit lives with me, and he is giving me strength to go through life with dignity and honor—the strength that he couldn't find for himself during his own life. This strength has helped me recognize both the bad and the good in my family's legacy—the fact that while they may have been capable of terrible retribution against men like Scalise, Anselmi, and Gunita, they would never have been capable of killing innocent people, like on Saint Valentine's Day. I believe that, in a way, my father's spirit has helped me write this book.

7

Railroaded

I was willing to go to jail. I could have taken my stretch, come back to my wife and child, and lived my own life. But I'm being hounded by a public that won't give me a fair chance. They want a full show, all the courtroom trappings, the hue and cry, and all the rest. It's utterly impossible for a man my age to have done all the things I'm charged with. I'm a spook, born of a million minds.
- Al Capone

The tides changed for Al Capone after the Saint Valentine's Day Massacre. Before that day, Chicago had been willing to tolerate him—even smile upon him—because, whether it was illegal or not, the people wanted what he was selling.

As Al himself said, "Nobody wanted Prohibition. This town voted six to one against it. Somebody had to throw some liquor on that thirst. Why not me? I give the public what it wants. I never had to send out high-pressure salesmen. I could never meet the demand."

But after February 14, 1929, all that seemed to change. The newspapers were full of accusations, and the public was quick to react. No one wants to live in a lawless town, and Al Capone had come to symbolize recklessness and an utter disregard for order that went unchecked by the authorities. Of course, the police, lawmakers, and judges would probably have been happy to continue turning a blind eye to the Outfit's operations indefinitely because they benefited from the speakeasies in payouts, booze, and good times. But once the public, spurred on by the media, was in a furor, the leaders of Chicago sensed they had to put a stop to Capone—or risk losing their power.

Uncle Al was not slow to notice the cooling of temperature. And as much as this worried him for himself and his business, he was doubly worried for his family. Family was everything to him, and when he saw that his mother, wife, and son would suffer for his activities, he was deeply troubled.

Al said. "I've got a mother who never misses mass unless she's too sick to get out of bed," and "I've got a wife who loves me as dearly as any woman could love a man. They have feelings. They are hurt by what the newspapers say about me. And I can't tell you what it does to my twelve-year-old son when the other school children, cruel as they are, keep showing him newspaper stories that call me a killer or worse."

To make matters worse, Al's success was a threat to other businessmen in Chicago. He wasn't just hounded by the public and the law, but other businessmen—both legitimate and racketeers—were doing everything in their power to push him out. He was the biggest competition there was. At the end of the 1920s, he was at the pinnacle of his success. The Outfit brought in more than $100 million a year, all of it cash. Most of his business centered on selling beer, liquor, and prostitution, but he and his cronies also owned and operated gambling establishments, dog tracks, dance halls, roadhouses, and other resorts.

A powerful, unofficial ruling party of businessmen in Chicago, called the Secret Six, began to feel they had to do away with the Al Capone competition at all costs. The Chicago World's Fair was looming large. Scheduled for 1933, the city expected the fair to draw millions and be a major source of revenue. The Secret Six did not want Al Capone encroaching on their profits. But he would surely be in the spotlight throughout the event, and so he had to be eliminated before it opened.

The Secret Six was led by the owner of the *Chicago Tribune*, Colonel Robert Rutherford McCormick. In the *Illinois Public Journal*, Burton Cooke wrote of Colonel McCormick's vendetta against Al: "McCormick was a person who followed his own conscience, whether right or wrong, and used his paper to shape public opinion. He aroused the public with numerous newspaper articles, most of them inaccurate, to put pressure on the police and politicians to break Al Capone's hold on Chicago and put him in prison."

The trouble for the Secret Six was that they couldn't make any aggressive moves against Al because they had to keep him quiet. He had the dirt to implicate three-quarters of the Chicago political and business establishment in his criminal activities—and no one doubted that if he went down, he'd take all other guilty parties down with him.

Luckily for the Secret Six—and unluckily for Uncle Al—the perfect opportunity arose. Though he was squeezed from all sides by law enforcement, the media, and the public, and though he was being accused of heinous and innumerable monstrosities, it was actually a very minor offense that provided law enforcement with the right excuse to move in on Al.

In 1928, Uncle Al—under the false name of Parker Anderson— purchased a home on Palm Island near Miami for $40,000. Members of the Outfit loved to go down there during the winter months and play. You can imagine the noise that went on late into the night at that house. Unbeknownst to Uncle Al and my grandfather, the next-door neighbor hated the partying and called the police a couple of times. Of course, the police did nothing because the chief of police was frequently one of the partiers. So, this neighbor, who worked for the federal government, took his complaint to the next level. He phoned a friend of his—who just happened to be President Herbert Hoover.

President Hoover's response was, "Get Capone!"

"Get Capone!" became a battle cry throughout America. As Al described it, "Every time a boy falls off a tricycle, every time a black cat has gray kittens, every time someone stubs a toe, every time there's a murder or a fire or the Marines land in Nicaragua, the police and the newspapers holler, 'Get Capone!'"

At that point, any excuse would do to put him away. President Hoover had a friend in the Treasury Department named Frank Wilson. He was the one who first came up with the idea of looking into Al's tax files—and he found that Al owed some back taxes. In fact, Al had offered to pay up on a number of occasions, but could never get the IRS to give him a clear total of how much he owed.

Both the theory and practice of taxing income were significantly different in the early 1920s from what we know today. Today, just about everyone lives with the understanding that income taxes are a given and that willing tax evasion is a fairly serious offense. But income tax was still quite new when Al was operating the Outfit.

In 1913, the Sixteenth Amendment to the Constitution made income tax a permanent fixture in the United States. This Amendment represented a significant ideological shift for most Americans. Since the Boston Tea Party more than a century earlier, taxation had been a hot-button issue in America, and many felt that any form of taxation was an infringement on their inalienable right to liberty. The income tax, therefore, was very difficult to institute, and it has taken a lot of time to evolve to the significance it now holds in our financial lives.

When Al Capone was charged with tax evasion, income tax laws were relatively unknown, misunderstood, and neglected by the overwhelming majority of U.S. citizens. People were not even required to file if they earned less than $5,000 a year—an income bracket that represented more than 90 percent of the population. Al obviously was bringing in more than $5,000 a year, but there was a provision in the income tax law that stated that one did not have to declare any income made illegally—such as from gambling or bootlegging—because to do so would be self-incriminating.

The government was also not particularly diligent about pressing the issue of owed taxes. They did not send out personal income tax forms as they do today, and tax law was still obscure enough that most people who did file needed the help of an accountant or lawyer. Today, it's hard to imagine being ignorant of one's obligation to pay income taxes, but in 1931, most people actually were—and the government understood this.

So, when the federal government indicted Uncle Al in 1931 with twenty-one felony counts of tax evasion for the years 1924 to 1929 and two misdemeanor counts of failing to file a tax return for 1928 to 1929, everyone—from the government itself to the media to the public to Al and the family—understood this to be a strategic maneuver. At first, Al was not even particularly worried. Seriously punishing anyone for tax evasion was almost unheard of. Moreover, Al was still confident he had the judges in his pocket—and he paid off his jurors.

What he didn't bank on was the vehemence of the public outcry against him—made all the more heated by persistent media accounts of his guilt. And he also underestimated the wiliness of the Secret Six. They hired witnesses to lie on the stand and falsified evidence to help the prosecution. They even went so far as to bribe Al's lawyers to do a shoddy job. My grandfather Ralph told me that after Al's trial and a series of appeals had concluded, the lawyers returned all of the money the Outfit had paid them for Al's defense and admitted their corrupt dealing with the Secret Six.

Uncle Al didn't stand a chance. On Saturday, October 10, 1931, my whole family gathered at the Prairie Avenue home to prepare a big feast. They were certain that when the jury returned its verdict, Al would come out on top. At best, he would be found not guilty on all counts, and at worst, he might have to serve two or three years.

But Al's luck had run out. At the conclusion of his eleven-day trial— more a show than an honest inquiry into his guilt or innocence—he was convicted on three counts of tax evasion for the years 1925-1927, as well as two other misdemeanors. Only thirty-two years old at the time, he was sentenced to eleven years in prison—ten to be served in a federal prison and one in a county jail—and fined $80,000 in back taxes and court costs.

To give you a comparison, two years before, my grandfather Ralph was also convicted of income tax evasion for the same years, but was only sentenced to three years imprisonment. He served his time in the Federal Prison at McNeill Island in Washington. Frank Nitti, one of Al and Ralph's associates, only received an eighteen-month sentence for his tax evasion conviction. And Jake Guzik, another member of the Outfit, received a five-year sentence—and it's likely that even this comparatively short sentence was lengthened by the falsified testimony of Fred Ries, who probably was also paid by the Secret Six to lie in Al's trial.

When he was convicted, Al said, "I'll be made an issue in the next presidential campaign. 'We sent Capone to the penitentiary,' they'll be saying. It wouldn't seem so bad if they didn't use the income tax for political purposes. There's a lot of big men in Chicago who beat the government out of most of the taxes they ought to pay, and they get away with it. I don't think that's playing fair, but they've got me, and I'll have to take the medicine."

Al's lawyers immediately filed an appeal, and while it was pending, Al was incarcerated in the Cook County jail. He continued to run the Outfit from prison, and my grandmother and aunt brought him meals almost daily. He spent eleven months in Cook County waiting for the results of his appeals—but those eleven months did not count toward the completion of his eleven-year sentence. Of course, according to my grandfather, because his lawyers had been paid off, the appeals ultimately concluded unsuccessfully in 1932, and he was then transferred to the Atlanta Federal Penitentiary.

As soon as Al was processed in Atlanta, he filed for a writ of habeas corpus (statute of limitations). The writ of habeas corpus is a summons with the force of a court order sent to the warden of the prison, where the prisoner is residing, demanding that the warden bring the prisoner back into court with proof that the warden has lawful authority to hold the prisoner. It is a tool that has historically been an important instrument for the safeguarding of individual freedom against arbitrary state action. Had it been successful it would have thrown out several conviction counts and required a new substantially reduced sentence. Uncle Al knew by then that the Secret Six had paid off his lawyers, and he wanted to appear in court with new lawyers to present this new evidence.

The authorities did not want to run the risk that Al's petition might be successful. They nabbed him under tenuous enough circumstances, and if he got a re-trial with proper lawyers, there was a good chance he could get off. He'd be right back in Chicago again—and they wanted to avoid that at all costs.

The answer was to cut off his last legal recourse. He already exhausted the appeals process, making the writ of habeas corpus his last shot at freedom. If they could keep him from filing for the writ, they could keep him locked up. And that's exactly what they did.

At that time, prisoners in certain maximum-security federal prisons were barred from petitioning for a writ of habeas corpus. The argument was that they were so dangerous that it was a risk to bring them out of prison and into court. So, the solution to Al's petition for a writ of habeas corpus was to put him away where such a writ would be void. The solution was to send him to Alcatraz.

Al Capone's cell at Alcatraz

Alcatraz

I leave with gratitude to my friends who have stood by me through this unjust ordeal, and with forgiveness for my enemies. I wish them all a Merry Christmas and Happy New Year.
- Al Capone

In 1934, the facilities on Alcatraz Island in San Francisco Bay were repurposed. The island had belonged to the U.S. military for nearly a century, and since the Civil War, its buildings had been used to incarcerate military personnel. In the summer of 1934, however, not long after Uncle Al's last appeal failed, Alcatraz began serving as a federal maximum-security prison for civilian offenders.

The new warden of Alcatraz, James A. Johnston, under the direction of J. Edgar Hoover, wanted to create a mystique surrounding the prison. He wanted it to instill fear in the hearts of the lawless and a sense of security in the law-abiding. He wanted it to be "The Rock"—a place from which no man could escape.

What he needed was media attention. The island was already remote, the facilities well fortified. All that remained was to make sure people knew it. And, as the previous decade had proven, few men were as sure a draw for media interest as Al Capone. If the authorities tossed Al in Alcatraz and threw away the key, that would give Johnson a victory to boast about. He could claim that Alcatraz was responsible for keeping America safe from a menace. Warden Johnston's interest in Al coincided neatly with my uncle's petition for a writ of habeas corpus, and so Alcatraz became the best solution for everyone—except, of course, Al.

Before Alcatraz opened, Director of Prisons James Bennett visited other prisons and told the warden at each prison to give him a list of their "worst offenders" and then he personally chose the convicts to be transferred. Everyone transferred from other federal prisons had reputations as troublemakers, men who had tried to escape, and men who did escape but were later caught—everyone except for my uncle. Al was only transferred to Alcatraz for the publicity. There was no other reason for such an extreme decision.

News of his transfer was published in newspapers around the world. Articles called Alcatraz the place where the most violent and dangerous criminals in the country were held. Al's name appeared alongside those of serial killers, bank robbers, and escape artists. I personally believe that his transfer to Alcatraz marked the true beginning of my family's reputation—real or imagined—for ruthlessness.

Warden Johnston spent much time studying the procedures of other prisons—both federal and state—in the United States. From his personal study and observations, he and his staff selected rules and regulations they deemed suitable to maintain order among the dangerous men incarcerated at Alcatraz.

When I learned of the conditions that the prisoners in Alcatraz were subjected to, I was appalled. These rules would almost certainly not stand today, but were commonplace in all prisons at that time. "Cruel and unusual" does not even begin to describe them. It's no small wonder that some men took big risks to escape. In the magazine *American Mercury*, Anthony M. Turano published an article called "America's Torture Chamber," in which he wrote that Alcatraz existed solely to inflict a "special social vendetta on the gangsters" and stood as a "monument to human stupidity and pointless barbarity."

Perhaps the most restrictive of the rules was the "Silent System," which Johnston borrowed from the Stillwater Penitentiary in Minnesota. The Silent System, as it was enforced at Alcatraz, seemed to be the nucleus of all the unrest, trouble, and violence that happened there. Inmates were forbidden to speak while in their cells, the cell house, dining room, or wherever they gathered in the main buildings, whether in the shower room, clothing room, sick cell, or court call. New inmates in Alcatraz became functionally proficient in sign language within a few days. Mostly everyone communicated with his hands.

Upon entering Alcatraz, each man was given a number, and from that moment on, it became his identity. He was that number. He was addressed by it, he answered to it, and all papers concerning him were marked by it. His mail, clothes, shoes, cell, and place of work were associated with it. It was a number every prisoner would remember until the day of his death—everyone except for Uncle Al.

Only Al's mother, wife, and son had permission to visit. My grandfather Ralph was barred entry because he was a convicted felon. The trip to San Francisco from Chicago by train took several days and was a significant expense, but Grandmother Theresa and Aunt Mae tried to coordinate their visits so that Al had as much time with them as possible.

The first visitors were Aunt Mae and Sonny. Sonny was still a boy at the time, and seeing his father in such horrendous conditions was a life-changing experience for him. He was a teenager raised in luxury by a very protective and kind mother and educated in a private school built with his father's dollars. His father had once been king of Chicago and the social czar of Miami, and now Sonny had to see him reduced to a life unfit for any human being. Many years later, Sonny himself told me about his experience at Alcatraz with tears in his eyes.

The next visitor was my grandmother Theresa. She, first, had to write a letter to the warden, giving the desired date of the visit. At the age of sixty-six, she traveled by train alone across the country to the San Francisco dock and took the ferryboat across the cold waters to the island. When she wrote with her requested visit date, she could not have predicted how the weather would cooperate. Unfortunately, on that particular day, there were high winds across the Bay that rocked the ferry violently. She was frightened and intimidated, but she was also a woman who had endured much in her life and was determined to see her beloved son. When the ferry docked at last, she had to climb a long flight of steep stairs, check her coat and baggage, and go through a metal detector. The alarm went off in the detector, and she had to bear the humiliation of a body search. A metal stay in her corset set off the alarm.

Once she got to the room to see her son, # 85, she had to sit on a chair facing a metal wall with a very small window. There were slats below the window through which she could hear his voice, but only see a small part of his face. He tried to move over as much as possible to let her see his eyes. She told me that, after the visit, she cried and prayed the rosary all the way back to Chicago.

Between visits, the entire Capone family kept in touch with Al via letters. But even their correspondence was restricted by the rules of Alcatraz. A prisoner was never allowed to read a handwritten letter. The prison staff would read every letter written to a prisoner, and then someone in the office would type it out and give it to him. This was a precaution against coded messages concealed in the letters, but seems cruel to imagine not being able to see the handwriting of a loved one or detect their scent on the page.

Prisoners themselves were only allowed to write one letter a week, and again, only to immediate family members. These, too, were reviewed by the prison staff. I can only imagine the gossip. They knew everything about every prisoner and probably used it against them when needed.

The following is a copy of a letter than aunt Mae sent to uncle Al. You will notice the reference to my Dad.

Capone ------- 85   4-15-37

My Dear Husband:

It is now three-thirty in the afternoon. Brown just came home with Joan but sonny stayed at school to play some handball. Brown will go after him later. He is just fine dear and doing nicely in school.

This morning Sonny received a letter from some friends of Ralphie's. A very nice letter concerning Notre Dame. Sonny and I appreciated it but as far as Sonny is concerned he will choose his own college on its own merits and as he prefers it. He is like that doing things for him-self. Goes places that he can get into and wants to be liked for him-self. Of course it doesn't hurt to have everyone to say a nice word for one and I know that Ralphie's friends will do that for Sonny but Sonny has never needed help before and has made all his grades without aid, has been liked and respected by all because he is a good boy and does respect the rules and regulations and doesn't think that he knows it all. I am sure that he will get by dear. The Nuns and Priests think the world of him and parents of the school children would rather have him around with them than anyone else. Dear, it is just the narrow minded people that cannot think that run people down, without knowing what they are doing it for.

We have nothing in this world to be ashamed of and we are proud of our Daddy so I want our son to go out in the world, face all, let all know who he is and accept him for what he is. There will be many obstacles that will face him during his life and I am sure that he will face them and be better thought of in the end.

Oh Darling, I could go on forever writing about things that I have in my mind but I know that you understand how I feel and what I want our son to be a respected man by all, just for himself for he has his life to live and deserves a chance like everyone else in the world so I never discourage him in anything that he wants to do, but shall help him always. No one has worried about his success or welfare before so I don't expect it. We'll get by.

Well sweet, I hope that you are OK. After all there are but two people in this world that I worry about and live for and those are my husband and my son.

God Bless you – I love you Love and kisses – Always,

Your wife and son.

X X X X X X X X X X X X X X X X X X X X X X X X X X X X X X X X X X X X X X X

Despite these tight restrictions on his correspondence, according to Johnny Chase, (see his letter in the appendix) Al did manage to get cash delivered to him by the Outfit, which he divided up into several batches of $500. He hid these batches in different parts of the island where they were accessible to inmates who had gained his trust.

Among the inmates who knew of Al's hidden money was Roy Gardener, # 110. He was an escape artist and, along with my uncle, among the very first men to arrive at Alcatraz on September 2, 1934. Roy began planning an escape and tried to get Al to be part of it. When Al wouldn't go along with the plan, he was stabbed in the leg in the laundry room. But Uncle Al's money financed what was probably the only successful escape from Alcatraz in all its twenty-nine years as a federal penitentiary.

Over the course of those twenty-nine years, a total of 1,547 prisoners were incarcerated in Alcatraz. Thirty-four made fourteen separate escape attempts; of these, six were shot and killed, twenty-three were caught, and five were never found, and so were presumed drowned in the San Francisco Bay. But did they really die?

As I researched Uncle Al's experiences at Alcatraz, I came across some truly fascinating writing by one of Al's fellow prisoners, a man named Johnny Chase. I found a letter written to Father Clark by Johnny Chase.

Johnny was a rum-runner and had lived in the Bay area for many years. He was familiar with the Bay waters, knew all the roads around San Francisco where men could meet and hide, and he had associates living throughout California whom he could trust to assist him during and after an escape. Within the walls of Alcatraz, he was assigned to work in the machine shop, where all the essential tools required for an escape were available or could be made.

Johnny wrote that in the spring of 1937, two inmates named Ralph Roe, # 260, and Ted Cole, # 258, approached him wanting to discuss the feasibility of swimming to the shore from the island.

Ralph was from Muskagee, Oklahoma and had been in and out of the prison system since he was twenty years old. In 1934, when he was perhaps twenty-nine years old, he escaped from a prison and robbed a Federal Reserve System Bank. The money was never recovered, but Ralph was sent to Alcatraz. His friend Ted was an even shadier character. He was about twenty-three years old when he arrived at Alcatraz, but was first incarcerated when he was seventeen. During one of his stints in jail, he killed his cellmate, escaped, kidnapped a farmer, and forced him to drive him from Oklahoma to Texas. He was apprehended there and sentenced to fifty years in Alcatraz under the Lindbergh Kidnap Law.

Because they were constrained by the Silent System, their discussions often took place while they walked through the prison yard, or in muffled voices if they happened to find themselves next to each other in the bath line or on a "call-out," when the guards took roll.

Johnny describes these discussions in his writing. "In general, wherever the opportunity came or presented itself, we would exchange views and thoughts pertaining to the tides, their speed, and the drift towards or away from shore. Which was the best chance to take? Should we go with the incoming tide or the outgoing tide? Which way was the water traveling and when was it moving towards the ocean or in across the Bay towards Berkeley? How fast did the tide flow? How long a start would be needed?"

After many talks, the three men decided that, despite the cold, low tides, and faster currents, January was the best option because the fog would provide the thickest cover. Both Ralph and Ted were athletic and worked in their cells to keep themselves physically fit. The three men agreed that Johnny would help facilitate the escape but would ultimately remain behind.

The agreed-upon escape route was through the barred windows of the blacksmith shop. Johnny had stowed away hacksaw blades in places in the shop that the guards were unaware of, which they would use to open the bars. The men would then have to drop down to the catwalk that ran along the outside of the building and make their way about thirty-five feet to a gate, which was held closed by a huge padlock. They would need to break the lock by twisting it with a wrench. From there, they could reach the water.

The water, of course, was the major challenge. As Johnny writes, "Someone came up with the idea of using one gallon cans for water wings. This was a very good suggestion, and it is the one item that makes me believe that Ralph and Ted really made it ashore and got away."

These "water wings" are also how my uncle Al comes into play in the story. According to Johnny, both Ralph and Ted put sharp daggers in their cans and all their money. Johnny writes, "They had close to $400, most of it belonging to Capone (#85). Al Capone got into a swindle shortly before the escape plan began to develop. Capone had some money sent into the prison for him, which he divided into several batches of $500.... One of the fellows who had access to another $500 took it all for himself." That fellow was Roy Gardner, whom I mentioned above.

Johnny continues, "This $500, or what was left of it, about $375, was given to Ralph and Ted just before they left. I saw them put the money into one of the cans, then take it out and divide it, putting half in each. So each had half of the $375, plus some other money, plus the dagger."

Ralph and Ted prepared their bodies for the ordeal of swimming through the cold water by only wearing their prison-issue coveralls, which they were required to wear, and nothing else in the bitter winds, rain, and fog of the island. They would throw buckets of cold water on each other, and then walk around in their wet clothes until the guards noticed and made them change. They only showered in cold water, they only drank cold water, and they spent countless hours doing all the most strenuous exercises in the yard or in their cells.

In the blacksmith shop, the three men devised a scheme to condition the guard to not notice missing men when he took roll. While the guard was taking roll, one of the three prisoners would squeeze into a locker and hide. Just before the guard called in to report that his count had been off, the prisoner would slip back into rank, so that when the guard double-checked, he'd find that he had miscounted.

"This hiding out got to be quite a game," Johnny writes. "At first, the officer became concerned, then gradually he became accustomed to hunting one or two of us down, when we kept out of his sight by hiding in the locker." Finally, the guard "got to the point where he became lax."

Finally, on December 16 or 17, 1937, Johnny told Ralph and Ted, "Two days like today and yesterday are very rare. You'll never get fogs as dense as these." It was then or never.

The guard made his count and overlooked the missing men. Ralph and Ted smeared themselves with a thick layer of grease to protect themselves against the water, jerked out the blacksmith shop window bars, which they had quietly filed away for months, and slipped out the window with their "water wing" cans. Johnny, who had developed a relationship with the guard, managed to distract him and keep him from re-checking his men and sounding the alarm for nearly an hour and a half.

When the alarm was finally sounded, it appeared to everyone that the men had only been gone a few minutes, and so the search boats stayed close to the island. They performed an exhaustive search of all the small inlets carved into the island by the winds and tides. According to Johnny, they were looking in the wrong place—Ralph and Ted were far toward shore by then. Johnny and all the other prisoners were immediately confined to their cells, so Johnny could not keep an eye on the Coast Guard and F.B.I. boats patrolling the waters, but he didn't need to. He was sure his friends had made it.

"From all I can gather," he writes, "I would say that Ralph and Ted did make land and were in good shape. They had planned for everything that could conceivably happen.... I was informed that the gallon cans were found on the beach near Fort Baker. But I never heard anyone mention the finding of any money or the daggers that were in them.... The finding of the cans minus the contents leaves little doubt but that they did escape."

9

A Model Prisoner

*If Al Capone is found guilty, who is going to suffer—a masquerading ghost or
the man who stands before you? You're right; it'll be me…
Well, I'd much rather be sitting in a box watching the world baseball championship. What a life!*
- Al Capone

Although Al Capone had exhausted his appeals and was barred from petitioning for habeas corpus, he had one last recourse. There was a provision at Alcatraz allowing that a prisoner could get time-off for good behavior. My uncle became a model prisoner.

Father Joseph M. Clark, S.J., was the first clergyman at Alcatraz. He became a good friend to Uncle Al and was loyal and kind to my family. He would call my grandmother on a regular basis and tell her and Aunt Mae how Al was doing.

My grandmother would ask, "Does Al go to mass every day?"

Father Clark explained that there really was no place at Alcatraz for mass. She insisted that she wanted her son to go to mass each day. When Father Clark told Al about this, he asked if they could build an altar.

Father Clark found a room outside the infirmary where they could build an altar, and he showed Al a bronze plaque of the Last Supper that he would like to see on the front of it. Uncle Al gave him money and the inmates built the altar, candlesticks and all, out of mahogany.

I gave the inmates a bronze plaque of the Last Supper and they built this altar, candlesticks and all, out of mahogany.

I can't say it was easy for Al to behave like a model prisoner. Here was a man in his thirties, who had lived a life of splendor and could get just about anything he wanted. Now he was in a cell where his only thoughts and prayers were to get out and go home to his family. The prison officials did all they could to make him angry, but he wouldn't break. He would pray with Father Clark for strength.

On December 18, 1938, Uncle Al wrote in a letter to Aunt Mae, "I just came back from church. Father Clark had another priest here who just came back from Italy, and he gave us a good sermon all about Italy and Germany. In the meantime, dear heart of mine, please do not worry about me as I am improving every day. I get two treatments a week, and they do not hurt me at all. I work out in the recreation yard five days a week and Saturday and Sunday. I catch up on my music and read a number of monthly and weekly magazines and a hot bath every day and three good meals each day. I hope to see you and Sonny again before I leave here next January the 18th. I have quite a number of songs written for him to sing them to you, and I will play them on the piano or Mandola. Get in touch with my dear brother

Ralph, and for him to arrange to pay that $37,000 fine and costs I have to pay here, and then I can go to the Cook County jail. I will have to pay another fine there of $10,000. But when I come there I can see you and all of our dear family every week and I'm through with that sentence. Never again will I do anything to keep me away from you."

A short time later, in early January 1939, the prison officials told my family that Al started to exhibit unusual behaviors and had to be transferred to Terminal Island, a federal institution in Long Beach, California, where he was provided with medical care until he was released on November 16, 1939.

Just before his parole, Father Clark called my family and said, "They are destroying Al. They are giving him drugs in the infirmary, and he has lost his memory. He can't even remember my name."

By the time Al was released from prison at the age of forty, he was a shell of his former self. He spoke in a whisper as a result of the years of silence he endured in Alcatraz. He had trouble moving due to the prison stabbing. And he had suffered severe memory loss. He had no memory of Alcatraz and could not remember his number, a simple # 85. I have to wonder what kind of "medical care" he had on Terminal Island.

Contrary to what has been written, Al's health did not fail solely as a result of syphilis. I believe that his rapid decline was due to the torture he was subjected to in Alcatraz. Our family knows this because we have the word of Father Clark, the priest who visited him there. Father Clark told Mae and other family members, "They tried to destroy his mind in prison, and they succeeded."

One of the guards' favorite techniques was to put my uncle in a cell called "the hole" and alternate the temperature every half hour from very cold to very hot. This was accomplished by opening a window that was located behind the radiator until his cell was very cold and then closing it again to heat up the cell once more. He was also injected with chemicals on Terminal Island, under the guise of syphilis treatment. The business and political leaders of Chicago did not want Al Capone to return to power. Locking him up for nearly a decade was not enough—they had to make sure that all traces of his former self were gone.

Even despite this harrowing treatment, Uncle Al continued to be a model prisoner. He was released after serving only seven and a half years.

When Uncle Al was released from prison in 1939, he came back to Chicago before retiring to his home in Miami. My grandfather Ralph arranged a coming home party for him in his beautiful two-flat. The entire family went to church together that day, and then went back to the house where tables were laden with wine, liquor, breads, cold meats, cheeses, and cookies.

Al's mind was gone. He could not appreciate his own freedom or his family's joy. He acted very inappropriately. He wandered around, not recognizing people, passing gas at will, and when he went to the bathroom, he left the door open.

He had no memory. He could not remember even the closest members of his family. In fact, he would go up to them over and over again asking who they were.

"Who are you?"

"I'm Maffie, Al."

"Who are you?"

"Maffie."

His deep, thick, resounding voice was reduced to a whisper, and he winced as if in constant pain.

Stunned and grief-stricken to see his brother in this state, my grandfather called a friend who suggested they take Al to the Psych Lab at Johns Hopkins in Baltimore, Maryland. Aunt Mae and my grandmother Theresa took him there together, and he spent over four months in the care of doctors who worked tirelessly to rid his body of all the poisons that were in him.

Over the years, I have tried repeatedly to obtain the medical records from Al's stay at Johns Hopkins. I was able to obtain the name of the psychiatrist who treated Al, but by that time, he had already passed away. I spoke instead with his wife, who is also a psychiatrist. She told me that both she and her husband respected doctor/patient confidentiality, even within their marriage. They did not discuss their cases in depth. But she did tell me that her husband was very concerned about Al's mental health and about the treatment he received on Terminal Island. As she put it, "Something was wrong. His condition was not typical of syphilis." She also knew that her husband and other doctors were administering treatments meant to "leach poisons from his body." That is how she described it.

The Al Capone who emerged from prison was different from the Al Capone who emerged from Johns Hopkins. They were able, to some extent, to reverse the effects of his mistreatment in prison. If his brain had really been ravaged by syphilis, no treatment could have reversed it.

Theresa, Mae, and Al were all still at Johns Hopkins on the day I was born in 1940. Uncle Al was designated to be my godfather, but because he was in the hospital Sonny stood in for him. Aunt Mae and Uncle Al did send my parents a beautiful layette and crib. I have the signed gift card in my baby book. Below are the two telegrams they sent to the hospital on the day of my birth.

CONGRATULATIONS
by WESTERN UNION

CBD354 11 SC=BALTIMORE MD
MR AND MRS RALPH GABRIEL=
ILLINOIS CENTRAL HOSPITAL=
A BABY GIRL NEW LIFE NEW LOVE AND NEW HAPPINESS LOVE=
AUNT MAE AND UNCLE AL.

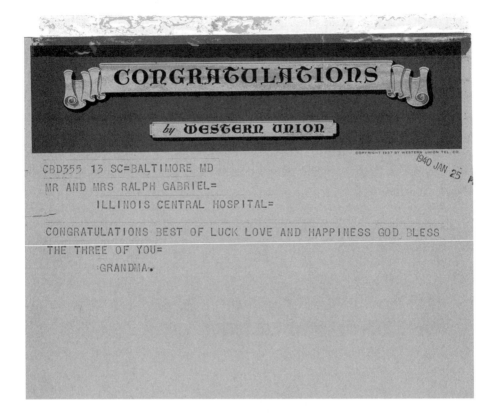

Aunt Mae took Al back to Florida to continue his recovery. With time, he recovered and was able to hold a conversation, but he always acted like a big kid. Even on the last day of his life, he couldn't remember being in Alcatraz or # 85.

———

At the time of Al's release, there was a newly-appointed U.S. attorney, Judge William Campbell, at the federal courthouse in Chicago. He wanted to make a name for himself, and Al Capone's crimes were still noteworthy and fascinating to the public. So he looked into whether Uncle Al ever paid his fine and court costs after his trial and conviction. Back in those days, if someone stood trial for anything and it resulted in a fine and costs, the courts usually sent a bill and then forgot about it—not unlike the federal government's laxity about collecting income taxes.

Judge Campbell saw that Uncle Al still owed the government money, so he filed to have Al stand trial again in Chicago.

When Uncle Al got the notice that he was to appear in court for a hearing, he called his brother, saying, "Ralph, take care of this, will ya?"

Ralph made a call to the Judge.

"Judge, this is Ralph Capone, Al's brother. Al wants me to come down there and give you the money he owes. Will it be alright if I come down there on Saturday at ten in the morning?"

Saturday at 10 a.m., two delivery vans pulled up in front of the courthouse. My grandfather went in the door and asked the deskman to get Judge Campbell. The judge instructed the deskman to send my grandfather up with the money.

The desk man replied, "I don't think that's possible, Judge. I think you better come down here."

Judge Campbell went down, and my grandfather took him outside where he opened the back of each delivery truck. It was filled with bags of pennies.

In 1939, people didn't put coins in paper rolls; all coins were loose. My uncle owed $47,000—or four million, seven hundred thousand pennies. Judge Campbell could not mark Uncle Al's debt paid until the pennies were counted. He himself said that he spent the next two days counting, then finally got fed up and hired people for the sole purpose of counting those pennies.

All the money was there, and the debt was paid. But because of this experience, Judge William Campbell, U. S. attorney for the federal government, attempted to get a statute passed that would make it impossible to pay taxes with coins. Although this was a popular belief, no such law was ever passed.

———

Upon Al's release, my family soon discovered that his memory loss would take more than just an emotional toll—there would also be serious financial consequences. Before going to prison, Al had hidden his money, which he kept in cash. And now, he could not remember where it was.

Many years after Al's death, I was asked to appear on Geraldo Rivera's television program when he famously opened the "Capone vault" on live television. I declined because I already knew the vault would be empty. Long before, in one of our many conversations about our family history, my grandfather Ralph had told me definitively that the money was lost forever.

"The worst part of [Al's incarceration] was what it did to his memory," Ralph told me. "That was catastrophic. It changed his life, my life, your life.... It changed all of our lives.

Your uncle Al had an incredible amount of money, money he couldn't put into a bank account or openly invest. He didn't trust the stock market; he called it a 'game.' And he didn't trust anyone enough, even me, to help take care of the money. So the main thing he did was get safe deposit boxes in various banks around the country and in Cuba, using assumed names.

After he was convicted of income tax evasion and was in Cook County jail, he confided to me that he had safely tucked away about $100 million, but he wouldn't tell me where he stashed it.

'Don't worry,' he said. 'Mae and Mom have enough to get by until I get out, and the Outfit is paying for my appeal. I will be out soon and then we'll all be in great financial shape.'

I had enough to take care of myself, so I didn't worry about it," Ralph continued. "But about a year or so after Al got out of prison, I was running short of cash, so I asked Al to lay some on me. You know what he said? He said he couldn't give me any right then.

'How come?' I asked.

'I'm a little low on funds, too.'

'What are you talking about? What about the $100 million you had stashed?'

He just looked at me. He had this pathetic helpless look on his face and said, 'Ralph, I don't know where it is.'

'What do you mean you don't know where it is?'

He looked down and shook his head. 'I don't know where the fuck it is.'

'Well, what happened? Why don't you know where it is?'

'I put it in a bunch of different banks and had the safety deposit box keys and the names I used in a strong box. I buried the box, but when I went to dig it up after I got out, I couldn't find it. Then I thought I had buried it in another place but when I looked, it wasn't there either.'

I noticed that there were tears rolling down his cheeks. Al was crying. I hadn't seen him cry since the cops killed our brother Frank on the street in Cicero. I tried to comfort him, but I was very upset myself.

Deirdre, we're talking about a fortune here. That was enough to take care of all of us for our entire lives. And suddenly, it was gone. There went our financial security. There went your college tuition. Poof! Just like that.

I did everything I could do to help him remember. I hired a hypnotist to see if he could pull it out of his subconscious. Nothing! I got Mimi, Bites, and Matty to help me dig up the yard on Prairie and his estate on Palm Island in Miami—again, nothing.

I don't know if this loss of memory was due to the syphilis. I don't think it was. I think it was because of what those prison docs did to him in Alcatraz. But either way, we're out a hundred million bucks. We used to make more than that in a year, but those days are gone forever."

Ralph sighed. "Sorry, Deirdre," he said. "I know I promised you that you'd never have to worry about money. But I can't help you now. If you're gonna be wealthy, you'll have to do it on your own, or marry a rich guy."

Certificate of Baptism

CHURCH OF

St. Anthony

Cicero, Ill.

THIS IS TO CERTIFY

that *Deirdre Marie Capone*

child of *Ralph*

and *Elizabeth Marie Boroloux*

born in *Cicero, Ill.*

on the *25d* day of *January*, 1940

was **BAPTIZED**

According to the Rite of the Roman Catholic Church

on the *2d* day of *March*, 1940

by the Rev. *Julian Grimis*

the sponsors being *Albert Capone*

and *Catherine Cavanaugh*

as appears in the Baptismal Register of this Church.

Dated *November 18*, 1950

Rev. *S. Albornoz*

JOHN P. DALEIDEN CO.-CHICAGO

10

The Capone Cabin
Mercer, Wisconsin, 1940 – 1947

I want peace, and I will live and let live. I'm like any other man. I've been in this racket long enough to realize that a man in my game must take the breaks, the fortunes of war.
- Al Capone

After Al Capone was released from Johns Hopkins in 1940, shortly after my birth, he retired to his estate in Miami. Although he looked healthy and strong, and his mind had begun to improve, everyone in the Capone family—especially my grandmother—knew that he was not the man they had known before he was sent to Alcatraz.

Theresa wanted him to heal in relaxing surroundings. She was very determined to take good care of him and to cook the foods that she was sure would make him healthier. And she didn't want him to be alone in Miami. My grandfather Ralph owned several properties in Mercer, Wisconsin, a small town 375 miles north of Chicago. He decided to purchase another hundred acres on Big Martha Lake in Mercer and build a huge log cabin for Al there.

In addition to the cabin, Ralph also owned the Rex Hotel, Billy's Bar, and Beaver Lodge in Mercer. I have so many childhood memories of those three establishments, and of Al's cabin. Much of the time I spent with Al Capone in the last years of his life was in Mercer, Wisconsin.

Ralph called the Rex a "hotel," but the rooms were generally rented by the hour, if you know what I mean. Billy's Bar was located in downtown Mercer and had a few key things in common with the Rex. One night when I was very young, I became tired while spending the evening with my grandfather at Billy's, and he asked a bar girl to put me to bed in one of the upstairs rooms. I realize now that the woman who maternally tucked me in bed that night was a prostitute who worked for my grandfather.

At the time, though, I thought nothing of it. The innocence of children is wonderful.

Billy's had a lot of the atmosphere of Al and Ralph's Chicago clubs—they insisted on good music and good times. There was an entertainer who sang and played guitar there often, named Marty Grey. He was the son of Gilda Grey, the girl who created the "shimmy," a popular dance in the 20s. He also emceed a weekly radio program, and when I visited my grandfather and Al in Mercer, Marty would let me come on the show. He would introduce me to the radio audience, and together we would sing duets.

The first time I can remember being at Al's cabin was when I was about four, just when my parents ended their marriage. My dad brought me there on the train, and Ralph picked the two of us up from the station. We drove down the highway from town and then turned right onto a dirt road. When we reached the edge of his property, Ralph unlocked a padlocked fence and, after we had passed through, painstakingly re-locked it. The entire compound was protected by a dense forest on one side and the lake on the other. At night, armed guards and dogs patrolled the area.

We drove down a long, winding, isolated road, flanked by birch and pine trees. The car headlights made the birch trees appear white, as if they were carved from ice. We then emerged into a large, open parking area in front of a rugged-looking, knotty pine log mansion. I thought it was one of the most beautiful homes in the world. I loved living there and still miss it to this day.

We parked in the two-story, three-car garage, above which the Outfit maintained offices. A "caretaker," who always carried a rifle or a revolver, was stationed in a room in the forward section of the garage. When we got out of the car, we entered the house through a door to the side of the garage door. Just inside the door was a corridor with a bathroom on the left. I still remember the Sears catalog hanging on a string near the toilet in that bathroom; I was enchanted by all the pictures of merchandise in it.

The aroma of liquor, cigars, and wood saturated the air as we walked down the corridor. The next room we entered had a long, wooden bar at one end with twelve stools. Shelves on the rear wall were laden with bottles of liquor. Beer and soda were kept cool in a small refrigerator under the bar. Among the many gadgets lining the bar, I remember most vividly a little ceramic boy standing before a toilet who peed whenever I mischievously lifted the toilet seat! There also were tables for poker or checkers, two slot machines, a large dance floor, a player piano, and a jukebox featuring bubbles that floated up tubes when it played music. At the other end of the room, a flight of stairs led to the upper floor.

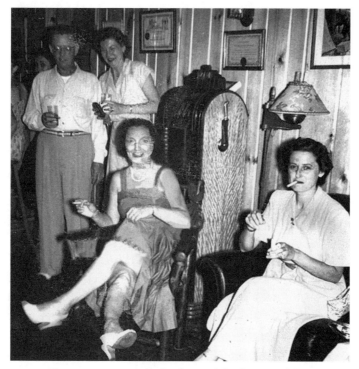

Guests at party in Lodge with slot machine

My cousin Sherman Hart is bartender, his wife Sis with my grandfather
Ralph at far end.

That first night, my father and I followed my grandfather upstairs.
When he turned on the light at the top of the stairs, birds—I thought,
though they were really bats—flew around and swooped down at us. Then
I saw the open mouth and shining fangs glaring out of the big white head
of a bear. It terrified me so much I fell backwards into my father's arms. He
picked me up and carried me ahead so that I could see it was only a huge
polar bear rug lying in front of the fireplace. But I was still so terrified
that they turned the rug away so I would not see the fangs the next time I
climbed the stairs.

A massive fieldstone fireplace dominated an entire wall of the huge
upstairs room and a wooden table at the other end could easily seat twenty
people. The ceiling was probably twenty feet-high. Leather chairs and
couches were pulled up around the fireplace and a moose head rested over
the mantle. The walls were built of knotty pine logs and held deer heads,
stuffed fish, deer feet holding rifles, snowshoes—and my picture, lovingly
hung there by my grandfather.

Fireplace with polar bear rug facing stairs.

Outside this room was an enclosed porch, which spanned the length of the building and overlooked Big Martha Lake—in fact, you could walk down a flight of stairs right to the water. At each end of the porch were big beds under the windows with curtains that could be pulled closed for privacy, like the sleeper car of a train. Each one was large enough to sleep four. I still remember we slept like that, two side-by-side and feet-to-feet, a couple of nights.

Deirdre Marie, 4, sitting on outside porch at lodge.

My grandfather's family and friends from the city often came to the lodge to unwind and then go into town to gamble. If we had a family reunion, as we did quite often for Uncle Al, some of the family would stay at nearby Beaver Lodge.

The log mansion was very much a male retreat, but I felt safe, secure, and wanted, and I stayed there many times for as long as three months at a time. When I did, the woman who was my grandfather's companion at the time had to leave. With Ralph, family always came first, and this was his way of letting these women know they were outsiders. They weren't allowed on the inside of the family—ever. When I stayed with him, hired help from the area cleaned and cooked for us. But when Grandma and Aunt Maffie were there, they did the cooking and I helped. They taught me dozens of culinary tricks and how to make many of the favorite family dishes that appear in this book.

I associate the log mansion with family. It was a warm, happy place, and only rarely did I catch glimpses of the other lives my uncle and grandfather led with the Outfit. But one thing that an outsider would have noticed as unusual was that there were no windows on the ground floor, in the big game room and bar. There were small skylights for light near the ceiling, but otherwise the only windows in the house were upstairs.

Playing in the master bedroom one day, I discovered secret rooms concealed behind panels in the closet. I touched what I thought was a wall, and it swung open. The instant it did, my grandfather appeared behind me and shouted, "Deirdre, what are you doing?"

He seldom raised his voice with me, but this time he was visibly upset. He pulled me out of the closet, looked me in the eye, and said, "Don't you ever go in there again! Do you understand?"

Fighting back tears and trembling, I said, "Yes Grandpa—er, Ralph. I understand."

"OK," he said. "Now go downstairs and play with your toys, and remember this part of the house is off limits." As I left the room and scampered down the stairs, I heard him say, "That's a good girl, Deirdre."

That was the last time I ever went near that closet. One of my cousins told me years later that he believed it was a staircase that went downstairs, underground, and into the garage. The house was way out in the middle of Ralph's vast property, and it was so remote and quiet there that it would be impossible to sneak up to it. You could see headlights coming from the main road and hear the car engine even before you saw the lights. You could hear the boats on the lake. You could almost hear a fly touch the water. So, my cousin thought this secret passage was an escape route. He is sure that, even today, if someone were to do an exhaustive search of the building, they'd still find relics of the Outfit in nooks and crannies in that house.

But these little reminders of the Capone profession were few and far between. Mostly, my time there was innocent and free. My grandfather Ralph always made room in his life for me, especially after the death of my father when I was almost eleven. My aunt Maffie told me that I was his favorite because I looked so much like his first wife, Florence.

I remember best the country drives we took along the back roads at night with the headlights of his station wagon off. He'd point out the constellations—the sky was always so clear in the country—and teach me the names of the different stars.

Al took me on one of these night drives once. He told me he wanted to show me something, and we got in the car and drove away from the lodge and down the main road. He parked the car in a wide field. There was a spotlight hooked up to the side of the car, and when he cut the engine, he aimed it out into the field and turned it on. The moment he did, all these deer appeared out of the darkness. He dragged it around the field, and the deer stood immobilized in the light—unable to run, but so beautiful.

"Deirdre," Al said to me, "some people use spotlights to kill deer. That's unfair. It's something you should never do, nor should you ever associate with anybody that would harm an animal unfairly."

Al and my grandfather were sportsmen and hunters. To them, hunting deer or other game to feed the family was honorable—but to shoot deer after immobilizing them was taking unfair advantage. These were the kinds of messages I grew up hearing from the Capones.

We spent summers fishing and swimming in Big Martha Lake. It was too weedy for swimming near our lodge, but on the other side, where our friends the Krumdicks lived, swimming holes were plentiful and we were always welcome.

The fishing was good. We usually caught northern pike, bass, and sunfish. Grandpa Ralph taught me how to filet the fish and we would bread them and pan-fry them while they were fresh. It was some of the best fish I ever tasted.

A loaded pistol and a rifle always accompanied us in the boat, and I was not allowed to touch them. My grandfather told me the pistol was there in case we caught a musky. He said they were so ferocious they could bite you when you got them in the boat, so we'd have to shoot them. Remembering that today, I have to laugh that I fell for it. I never saw anyone catch a musky, but I doubt you have to shoot them. That pistol was there for protection against much bigger threats than muskies.

The rifle, on the other hand, was actually there for a woodsman's reason. They kept it in case we encountered a bear. I never ran into one in the woods, but actually, a big bear did try to get into the lodge one night. It scared me half to death.

The grown-ups were having a party downstairs as I slept in one of the Pullman beds on the porch. I heard a scratching sound and went downstairs to tell my grandfather. He told me there was nothing to worry about and to go back to sleep. I went back to bed but kept hearing the same sound—getting louder by the moment. I again went downstairs, interrupting the party one more time. My uncle Bites got very annoyed with me and brought me upstairs with a flashlight. He made me stand up on the bed and look out the window. He planned to shine the light and show me that nothing was wrong. As he did, a big bear stood up on its hind legs and stared into the light. Bites let out a huge yell, "Holy Shit"! which brought my grandfather and cousin Sherman running. The bear took off, but it had been trying to claw its way into the house. The next day, the men tracked the bear, found it wounded, and shot it. When my grandfather told me about it, there were tears in his eyes.

My little brother, Dennis, who was four years younger, and I had great fun at the lodge in the winter, too. Ralph kept two reindeer in a stable on one side of the building, and in the winter, he would take us on enchanting sleigh rides around the surrounding acres. We built snowmen, made snow angels, sledded, skated, and hurled snowballs. We didn't know about cross-country skis in those days, but I did have my own snowshoes, which I used often.

On cold mornings in the lodge, Grandma poured hot sugared coffee into large cups half-filled with milk. Uncle Al would pick up a brown bag of Biscotti that he had baked the night before. We each took a cup of coffee and a few cookies and dunked them while eating in front of the fireplace in the living room.

Back in those days, listening to mysteries, comedies, and music on the radio were our only entertainment options. Some of my most memorable moments with Uncle Al were when my dad, Aunt Maffie, and I would prepare for an evening of radio.

We had a kind of ritual. We would always make popcorn first—in our own unique, Capone way. Al would bring out this big gunnysack, or burlap bag, filled with ears of popcorn. He had a farmer friend who grew popcorn, and he would bring a couple of these huge bags to him every year with the corn still on the cobs.

Popcorn, unlike sweet corn, is extremely hard and dry. We would remove the corn from the cob by holding an ear in both hands and then pressing our thumbs on an angle against the corn until it loosened and came off the cob. It took a lot of pressure to remove the corn, and I was just a kid, so I couldn't do it as well as Al, Maffie, or my dad, so they did most of the work.

Uncle Al would then take a small pot, put in lard or Crisco, and heat it on the stove. He dropped in three kernels of corn and when those popped, he grabbed a big handful of popcorn and dropped it in the hot oil and put on the lid. The popping began almost immediately, and in a minute forced the lid up. Al put the pot over a large bowl and began to shake the popped corn out by lifting the lid to prevent the corn from flying all over, which it did anyway. He quickly returned the pot to the stove and the popping resumed. Believe me, we got many, many quarts of popped corn from that little pot. He kept this up until there were no more pops. He then emptied the pot and melted butter in it to pour over the corn. Finally, he sprinkled on the salt.

Then we would all sit down around the radio. One of our favorite shows was *Red Skelton*—though I thought as a girl that his name was "skel-e-ton." All of us thought he was so funny. Red created all these different characters, and each had a different voice and personality. One was Clem Kadiddelhopper, a kind of simple country bumpkin guy who came out with some really clever remarks out of nowhere. Another was a nasty little kid who was always getting into trouble. Red referred to him, in a form of baby-talk, as that "mean little kid' who would always say the same thing just before he did something mischievous: "If I dood it, I'd get a lickin." (Pause.) "I dood it!'"

Uncle Al's favorite show was *Fred Allen*. Some of Allen's humor was a little sophisticated for me at that age, so I didn't always get his jokes, but I laughed with the adults anyway. Once something struck Al as funny, he often started laughing so hard he couldn't breathe. He would wheeze when he laughed that hard, but one time it was different.

"Are you OK?" Maffie asked. "Are you OK?"

In a minute, he started breathing again, pulled out his handkerchief, and wiped his eyes. He laughed so hard he was crying. He really had us scared for a minute.

Al said "Now I know what they mean when they say 'I laughed so hard I thought I'd die.'"

After my father's death, I often went up to Mercer with Aunt Maffie, where she spent a lot of time reminding me of some of these stories, telling me about our family, and teaching me to cook. She taught me how to cook chicken and noodles, which was my dad's all-time favorite dish, and we baked biscotti—the Al Capone way. We also had popcorn, of course.

I found out later in life that after my father committed suicide, my grandfather offered to give my mother the lodge, but she said no because she didn't want to leave Chicago. That was only one of the many differences between my mother and me.

11

Dandelion Soup
Chicago, 1944

I've been spending the best years of my life as a public benefactor. I've given people
the light pleasures, shown them a good time. And all I get is abuse.
- Al Capone

My family had much to celebrate one sunny Saturday morning in April, 1944. The war in Europe seemed to be going well, and even as a small child, I could feel the optimism in the air. In fact, D-Day was only weeks away, and there was a sense of excitement that America was about to liberate the world from the tyranny of the Third Reich. The sudden warm weather in Chicago made everyone smile and, after a long, cold Chicago winter, the dandelions were pushing up through frosty flowerbeds.

I was especially grateful for those long, green-stemmed dandelions. All over Chicago, the spring-time sun tugged the slender stems upward. Their yellow petals hadn't yet bloomed, so that's when they stood tall for harvesting. If I ever picked a petaled dandelion and gave it to my grandmacita Theresa for soup, she'd refuse it, saying it was too late—all the plant's goodness had gone into growing the petals.

The air was refreshingly warm, and I wore a pair of sun shorts, a colored jersey, and play shoes. As my father and I walked down Prairie Avenue, we passed kids fooling around in their back yards. One boy threw a baseball against a brick wall and caught it in his mitt. I can still hear the loud thump as the ball hit the wall and the slap as it hit the boy's glove. Thump, slap. Thump, slap. Thump, slap.

I lived on Indiana Avenue and 71st Street in Chicago with my parents and infant brother in the rented first level of a two-story brownstone, where things were always tense between my parents. It was just a ten-minute walk from Grandma's house, but it may as well have been from one planet to another. Just a few months later, my parents would split up, and I would be left to live with a mother who always seemed to resent me.

In contrast, at the Prairie Avenue house, I was surrounded by warmth, the perpetual smell of cooking, and laughter. Money really did seem to grow on trees. The bill of choice at 7244 South Prairie was the hundred-dollar bill. One hundred dollars was a lot of money back then, according to inflation tables, $100 then was the equivalent of $1,440 today. My dad was always asking Al and Ralph for money, and I never saw either one of them pull from their pocket anything less than a hundred.

"Look, Dad!" I shouted happily that particular Saturday, showing him how my skipping technique had improved. I think there was an extra bounce to my step because I had his attention to myself, my mother having stayed home with my colicky brother.

"I'm going to pick dandelions today and help Grandmacita and Aunt Maffie make soup!"

My father caught up with me and smiled. "Save your energy. There will be so many dandelions in the yard, Grandma and Aunt Maffie won't be able to pick them all without your help."

"And we'll bathe them," I added. "I'm the only one who can clean dandelions right."

I hummed a popular song "Mairzy Doats" to myself as we approached the house, hopping up the nine front steps. I barely noticed the two burly men standing guard on the street, though they made no attempt to hide the machine guns slung over their shoulders. During those years, Uncle Al and Aunt Mae spent most of their time at their home in Palm Island, Florida, but whenever they were in Chicago, two or more bodyguards would appear.

"My brother is an important man," Aunt Maffie explained to me. "There are always bad men who want to hurt him."

But I wasn't scared. My family would keep me safe, as would my uncle Al. I certainly wasn't scared of guns, even machine guns. My grandfather Ralph had already given me a small pump rifle. With it, I would kill my first squirrel a few months later during a visit to the house in Mercer—though seeing that squirrel die upset me so much that I never shot another animal.

"Hi, Grandmacita. Hi, Aunt Maffie," I called out as I skipped down the long corridor to the kitchen. "Are you ready to pick dandelions?"

There were a few "jobs" that Grandma asked me to do for her. Picking dandelions was one and dusting under the dining room table was another.

The table was a heavy walnut table with ornate legs. Grandma and Aunt Maffie could not crawl under it like they used to, so that became my job almost every week.

A few minutes later, I was bent over in the wide grass yard with Grandmacita and Aunt Maffie. I was a lot closer to the ground than the two women, and because of that, I considered myself to be the best dandelion picker of all of us. Aunt Maffie insisted on bending at the waist, saying that picking dandelions helped to exercise her stomach muscles. Wisely, Grandmacita dropped to her knees to make it easier on her back. I simply plopped the dandelions into my apron, which I held with my other hand to form a bowl.

It took us about an hour to pick all we needed. Then we brought the dandelions to the upstairs bathroom. While Grandmacita filled the bathtub with cold water, we dropped our dandelions onto the water's surface. There, we let them soak for an hour while all the dirt sunk to the bottom. My job was to submerge the dandelions every fifteen minutes or so after they rose to the top.

"The stems have to be really clean or I can't make good soup," Grandmacita reminded me. She was always fussy about cleaning the dandelions just right.

Finally, we wrapped them in a wet towel and brought them back downstairs for Grandmacita to inspect. Grandmacita was very much in charge of her kitchen and, therefore, the household. After she died, at the end of 1952, nothing was ever the same, certainly not our Sunday meals. But at that time, she directed traffic. She was in the middle of preparing various dishes—a roast in the oven, water simmering on the stove waiting for the dandelions, fresh pasta hanging to dry in the pantry, and garlic, cheese, and onions laid out for chopping on the kitchen table.

Uncle Al was sitting in the kitchen with his mother when I came down. Grandmacita placed her hand on his head fondly.

"Deirdre has picked and cleaned the dandelions," she told him in her thick Italian accent. "What do you think about that, Al?"

Uncle Al smiled and kissed his mother's hand.

Of course, I had never heard of syphilis then, nor did I know the details about Al's imprisonment, but I remember noticing Grandmacita and the rest of the family's concern about Al's health. She always fussed over him, urged him to eat or drink soup or vegetables or even to take a shot of whiskey. She was a big believer in food as medicine, something passed down the Capone line for generations that I, too, have tried to impart to my children. When we prepared meals, she often said a prayer, her fingers trailing over the cross she wore or the rosary that always seemed to be folded in her hand.

"My spring-time dandelion soup will clean away the unhealthiness of winter," Grandmacita told Al. I'm sure she didn't know the scientific details then, but I have since discovered that in addition to vitamin A, calcium, potassium, and iron, dandelions also help cleanse the liver and eliminate toxins from the body.

While Aunt Maffie began kneading bread dough in the kitchen, Grandmacita and I went back outside. Uncle Al joined us, seating himself on the wooden bench near a flowering cherry tree. An apple tree stood at the other end of the yard. In the summers, Aunt Maffie—the baker in the family—would serve cherry pie, and in the fall, apple pie, both of which were made with the fresh fruits of these two trees. We ate the pies straight from the oven, but when she prepared fresh applesauce, we would can it and store it for the winter.

Grandmacita walked over to the bench, sat down next to her son, turned her pale face toward the warm sun, and closed her eyes. She still had a babushka tied around her hair.

Uncle Al looked at his mother and asked, "What are we having for dinner?"

Without opening her eyes, she said, "Dandelion soup, and your favorite, rump roast."

"Can I climb the tree and smell the blossoms, Uncle Al?" I asked.

"You really think you can climb that tree?" He asked with a smile and a wink.

"Just watch me," I said bravely. I reached up to a branch and climbed into the leafy arbor umbrella.

A few moments later, I was teetering from a high branch, hollering, "Hey, Grandmacita, Uncle Al, look at me." They shaded their eyes and looked up. I waved vigorously at them.

"Be careful," warned Grandmacita.

Suddenly, my foot slipped. I lost my balance and fell heavily to the ground, landing on my back. The air rushed from my lungs, and I gasped for breath, petrified to find that I couldn't inhale.

"Are you OK?" I heard Uncle Al's voice near me. I couldn't reply. I couldn't breathe. "Take a deep breath, and you'll be fine," he told me calmly. I remember the look in his blue eyes—a mixture of concern and bemusement. He reached down and swept me into his big arms, patting me gently on the back. Suddenly, I felt a rush of air return to my lungs. As soon as it did, I burst loudly into tears, my face muffled in his shoulder.

"She's OK," Al told Grandmacita.

My father peered through the open kitchen window. "What happened to her?" he asked.

"She just got the wind knocked out of her," said Uncle Al. "She'll be fine."

After I stopped crying, Uncle Al took my hand. "Come with me, Deirdre. I want to show you something." We walked up the stairs and he placed me on the big sofa in the living room. Uncle Al went into his bedroom and brought back something that looked like a tiny guitar.

"What's that, Uncle Al?" I asked.

"It's called a mandolin," he said, strumming a few chords. "I learned how to play it while I was in California a few years ago." At that time, I did not know what I know today—he meant Alcatraz.

Using the thick fingers on his large, powerful hands, he strummed each string with a small red pick, and began to sing:

My bambino
Go to sleep.
All the stars
Are in the sky
Ready to say goodnight.
And I know my baby's sleepy too.
So close your little, drowsy eyes
Mamma will say goodnight...
As she sings this lullaby to you.

Al Capone sitting on that sofa upstairs in the Prairie Avenue home.

Uncle Al had a soft, soothing singing voice. He never sang formally, but I think he must have been a tenor. He repeated the words of the song to me one line at a time, and asked me to repeat them back to him until I had them memorized. Then he handed me the mandolin, showing me where to place my fingers to strum the simple tune.

From a young age, Uncle Al told me, he loved music, beginning with the Italian operas Grandmacita would play on her Victrola record player. Later, as a young man in Brooklyn, he would tune to the opera broadcast on the radio, often humming along with his favorite arias.

I never wanted to leave that house that night, and they knew it. I think I sensed the discord between my parents. The Prairie Avenue home was a safe haven, a place where I could forget the tension and unease that had become all-too-familiar in my young life.

As she walked me to the large front door, Grandmacita handed me a bag of sesame cookies and rubbed my back where I'd fallen. I munched those cookies all the way home, nestled in my father's arms.

I looked up at him and whispered, "Daddy, I was really, really scared today. I couldn't breathe."

"Yes, I know," he said. "But Uncle Al took care of you. You're OK now, aren't you?" I gripped his hand more tightly.

"Yes, I am," I answered proudly. "I'm OK."

Before I ever picked dandelions again, my mother left my father.

Grandma Theresa with baby Dennis

One night not long after, my parents' fighting kept me awake. My dad was shouting and yelling, banging his fists on the wall. I tried hard not to listen, but after a while, my curiosity and fear overcame me, and I got out of my bed to peek out the door.

He was so angry, and my mother just sat at the table smoking a cigarette. I turned away from them. Through the window, snow fell to the ground quickly. It was probably the last snowfall of that spring, and it was also the last night I would spend in that house, the last night in my dad's house. I got in bed and cried myself to sleep.

"Deirdre, do you want to have breakfast with me before I go to work?" Dad asked softly, trying to wake me the next morning. My mind was thick with the night's fitful sleep. I wasn't sure I had heard him, and I buried deeper into my covers, trying to shut out the light.

My dad and I always had breakfast together. Mom didn't eat with us. In fact, it was always my dad and never my mother who fixed me breakfast. My favorite was cinnamon and sugar on toast. He would toast a piece of bread, put on lots of butter, let it melt and then sprinkle sugar all over the butter very slowly so the butter was absorbed. When that was perfect, he sprinkled on the cinnamon. When I bit into the toast, the sugared butter would ooze through my teeth. What a sweet memory.

I heard the front door close and jolted out of bed. I went to the door and saw my father walking down the steps. I hurried back to my bedroom, put on some shoes, and ran out the door trying to catch him.

The snow was deep, making it hard for me to run. I got to the bus stop too late. He was on the bus, and I don't think he knew I had followed him to kiss him goodbye as I always did before he went off to sell used cars on the corner of 73rd and Stony Island.

I made my way back home through the snow. My mom was still in bed and my brother was asleep in his crib. I got back into my bed to try to get warm.

"Come on, Deirdre, get up. We have things to do today." My mother's voice cut through my sleep, so different from my father's tone a short while before.

I crawled out of bed to find my mother going through her closet, putting her clothes into a suitcase. Then she started packing some dishes into boxes.

In a short time she had boxes of dishes and clothes in the middle of the living room. The doorbell rang, and there stood a man I knew as Eddie. He had his car parked in front with a trailer hooked up to the back.

He started loading the boxes onto the trailer.

"Mom, what's happening?"

"For heaven's sake, please leave me alone. You don't understand."

Eddie started putting our furniture and other belongings into the trailer. My mother told me to get in the back seat. When we pulled away from the curb I remember standing up and looking out the back window screaming, "Daddy won't be able to find us when he gets home."

My mother, brother, and I moved into my grandfather and grandmother's third floor apartment on Jeffery Avenue in the St. Philip Neri Parish. There we were, my mother, my brother—an infant at the time—my grandmother and grandfather, my great-grandmother, and me living in a one-bedroom, one-bathroom apartment.

My father was left alone. His love story with my mother had ended.

He grew up the young prince of the Capone family, while she was the darling of the Chicago elite. Dad was full of promise. He studied at St. John's Prep School in Minnesota, went to Notre Dame and Roosevelt, and got his law degree at Loyola. The Capones expected him to play the kind of role that John Fitzgerald Kennedy would one day play for his family. He was brilliant.

My mother, too, came from a very wealthy family. Her father was a real estate tycoon who owned most of the South Side of Chicago. She grew up in a large home with a butler and a maid. Her clothes were hand-made for her.

But in the 1929 stock market crash, her father—my grandfather—lost everything. Like many investors of that decade, he had bought stocks on margin. When the stock prices went crashing down, the investor had to pay up what was owed. In order to do that, my grandfather had to sell all his properties. He eventually had to ask my mother to leave the private school she attended and enroll in a public high school. She did not like that, so she quit school in 1935 at the age of sixteen.

My parents met shortly after in 1937, while my father attended Notre Dame. I believe my mother was largely attracted to him because she hoped, like everyone in his family, that he would become the Capone family lawyer—and restore for her the life she had once enjoyed. Just after they met, she followed him to Indiana and moved into his apartment at Notre Dame.

Her mother and father were furious and disapproved of her behavior and her choices. But, despite the disapproval, my parents married in Williamsport, Indiana, on March 29, 1938. The private ceremony was performed by a justice of the peace. On my parents wedding certificate, my mother listed her address as Warren County, Indiana, and her occupation as "house girl.

My Mother and Father 1938 on his sailboat. Maffie is facing my Dad.

Not long after, my father got into a fight at Notre Dame trying to protect his cousin Sonny from some bullies. The two of them were only a year apart in age, and the shy and often sickly Sonny idolized my father. He followed him to Notre Dame. But after the fight, they both thought it best if they left school and moved back to Chicago.

My mother and father moved into the Prairie Avenue house while my father attended Roosevelt University, where he got a B.S. degree in engineering. He then went on to earn a law degree from Loyola University.

I was born while my father was still at Loyola. As long as my father was a student, my grandfather Ralph paid all his bills—even the ones for my birth. He was still, however, an extremely prideful young man and looked forward to the day when he could take care of his family and take his place as patriarch of the Capones, instead of depending on them to take care of him.

But when he passed the bar exam, the Chicago Bar Association would not let him practice. They never gave a clear reason, but it seems clear that it was something akin to the insurance company's reason for firing me—an association with the Capones could be damaging. People would suspect my father of corruption, and the Chicago Bar did not want to invite suspicion.

A series of other failures followed. My grandfather set my father up in a legitimate business, but when the Chicago media got wind of it, they made the assumption and published the allegations that the business was just a means for the Capones to launder money. Rather than go against the rising tide of public opinion, the family decided to shutter the business. From that point on, 1945 until his death, my father was a changed man.

He was shattered. I was too young to know it at the time, but Aunt Maffie told me much later that my dad simply could not cope with the humiliation and the stymieing of not only his professional aspirations but also his ability to achieve independence and provide for his family. He began going away for long periods of time—once he took an extended trip to Florida to talk to Al.

My mother's dream was dashed along with her husband's. She did not have the skills necessary to help my dad build a life. He had to borrow money from his father and his uncle Al and work at a used-car dealership, and that income fell far short of what my mother hoped for him and for herself. There was still money coming into the family from the Outfit's gambling and prostitution businesses, but times were still much tougher than Ralphie had been accustomed to growing up. And, of course, Al's life savings had disappeared.

My grandfather Ralph was also a firm believer in individual agency. He wanted his son to "tough it out." He himself was a self-made person, and he believed in "like father, like son." The trouble was that he did not factor in how spoiled his son was as a kid, nor did he realize just how emasculated and small his son felt by his inability to gain a foothold in the world. If he wanted to make more than a modest living, my father's only chance probably would have been organized crime. Luckily, he shunned that, too. The Outfit did offer him a job, but after having Al and Ralph lecture him for decades about, "Once you are in, you can never get out," I think he was fearful of accepting it.

Many years of distance and bitterness between my parents finally culminated in their divorce. Just before my mother died, she told me the real reason why her and my father's marriage ended. Only a few years after I was born, Uncle Bites and Aunt Larry adopted a boy—as it turns out, he was really my half brother. My father had a little fling in Miami after being rejected by the Chicago Bar Association. The tryst produced a son. Again, my grandmother Theresa insisted he stay in the family—much to the chagrin of my grandfather Ralph. Other family members told me he said, "That's just what we need around here—another kid!"

When my mother discovered what happened, she started having 'flings' herself. The strain of these infidelities, coupled with my father's broken dreams, broke the marriage. My mother filed for divorce shortly after moving me and my brother to her parent's apartment.

Of course, the news of the divorce made all the papers—Capone scandals were still hot topics. My mother loved the publicity, but her family was livid. Her maiden name, Barsaloux, had been publicized, and immediately her extended family, embarrassed by the black mark of divorce on their otherwise well-respected name, cut ties with her.

I not only lost my father in that divorce, but I also lost my mother. She was a product of the "Flapper" generation, born in 1919, she grew up in an era when women were undergoing a huge transformation. They were bobbing their hair and raising their hemlines—not only on their skirts, but also in the backseats of their cars. Women's sexuality was no longer an embarrassing secret to be hidden and guarded, and many, like my mother, took the new-found freedom to the extreme. By the end of her life, my mother had been married seven times. She loved the party life, and did all she could to avoid the "boring" life of home and family.

When she left my father, she was still young and beautiful. And she now had the added allure of being the ex-wife of a Capone. She wielded this power and independence to her advantage, and from my little girl's eyes, it seemed to me that her life became one party after another.

I was four when my parents divorced, and my mother tried to enroll me in kindergarten to get me off her hands. The school administrators, however, told her I was too young and would have to wait a year. So, my mother left me in the care of her father when she wanted to disappear— often for many days. My maternal grandfather never did recover his dignity from the crash. He drank a lot and would take me to taverns with him during the day. Most of the time he would leave me in the backseat of his car while he went into the tavern with his buddies underneath the L tracks on 63rd street. I remember feeling scared. At least I survived, but I now know that neither my grandfather nor my mother wanted me. They wanted me gone.

I got ill that fall, very ill. The doctor thought it was my tonsils, so I was scheduled for surgery at Michael Reese Hospital in November 1944. I remember my mother taking me to the hospital and putting me in a room that had a bed with sides pulled up like a baby crib. In those days, you were in the hospital for a couple of days before surgery. On the operation day, my father came to be with me. When he arrived, my mother got angry, started an argument with him and left. My dad stayed with me as they took me into surgery.

I remember the bright lights, the mask coming down over my nose and mouth, and the sharp, chemical smell of the anesthetic. My next memory was seeing a very bright light, a light that I do not know how to describe—a light that beckoned and comforted, a sound, music, a feeling. A man, whom I believed to be Jesus, took my hand, and we walked through a tunnel. I could see and hear people at the end of the tunnel.

Then I heard my Dad call to me. I looked up at Jesus and said, "I have to go back or my mom will be mad at me."

"OK, this time you can go back."

Of course, when I woke up in the hospital room in 1944, I did not know what happened. I later found out that I had died. They now have a name for people like me. I am an N.D.E. person: someone who has had a Near Death Experience. Apparently, I did not have tonsillitis but an infection that caused me to bleed to death during the surgery.

The following spring, my mother again took me to register for kindergarten. The school only had one room with a class in the morning and a class in the afternoon. My mother wanted me gone for the whole day, so she asked the nuns if I could go directly into first grade. They tested me and I passed. I skipped kindergarten and started the first grade in September, making me the youngest student in my class. (I would not turn six until the following January)

I had to bring my lunch to school. Not one other child brought their lunch to school in those days—they all went home to their mothers at lunchtime. Even the nuns would all go to their convent for lunch. I was alone with only the school custodian, and he gave me the creeps. I remember other children making fun of me as I sat alone in the schoolroom with my sandwich and cried. Finally, when I reached the fifth grade, I could walk home, bringing my younger brother, who was in the first grade, with me. I would fix us soup or a sandwich and then take him back to school. I think I was among the first of the "latchkey kids."

Lunch was the least of my difficulties at school. I experienced rejection, ridicule, shame, and punishment. All forms of discrimination. I entertained thoughts of suicide many times. You must remember that in 1944, women did not get divorced. Mothers stayed home and were there when the children came home from school.

I went to a Catholic school, thanks to Aunt Maffie, where more than once, a kind nun would say, "You know, your mother is living in sin." Then I would return home to a cold family life. My mother had no interest in me, and to my grandparents, I was a reminder of my mother's mistakes. My grandmother was disgusted by the very existence of the Capones; she would not even allow me to talk about them or what I did during visits at the Prairie Avenue house.

Every night, I would pray to God, "Please bring my father back." What other chance did I have?

Dandelion Soup

2 pounds dandelion greens
½ cup olive oil
3 cloves minced garlic
1 medium onion minced
4 cups chicken stock
½ tsp salt
¼ tsp fresh ground pepper
½ cup freshly grated Romano cheese

Pick the dandelions in the spring of the year before their flowers appear, pulling them up so their roots stay attached. Wash them carefully in several changes of water to remove any sand and dirt embedded in the leaves.

Heat the olive oil in a heavy saucepan. Sauté the garlic and onion in oil until transparent. Add the greens and sauté for 5 minutes. Add the chicken stock, stir in the seasonings and cook over low heat, covered, for 30 minutes. Sprinkle with grated cheese before serving. Serves 4-6.

The Al Capone Family

Cordially invites you to dinner at their home on

Sunday at 1:00 p.m....and Thanksgiving, Christmas,

St. Joseph's Day, Easter and Mother's Day.

As guest of honor, you will receive our

treasured family heirloom recipes and pictures.

After dinner if you like, you may join Al and his brothers

In a high-stakes poker game in the dining room,

Or drift into the kitchen with the women

for some "girl talk", and juicy gossip.

We look forward to the honor of your presence.

Sincerely,

Deirdre M. Capone

12

Capone Family Dinner
Chicago, 1944 – 1947

The country wanted booze, and I organized it. Why should I be called a "public enemy?
- Al Capone

I lived two childhoods, really. Around my mother, life was cold and unloving. But when I went to the Prairie Avenue house to be with my dad and the Capones, I felt warm and enveloped in love. How strange to me, then, that it was the Capone name that Chicago seemed to shun.

We were a typical Italian family. In the Italian tradition, loyalty and allegiance to the immediate family members was paramount, and we adhered to strong customs. Sunday dinner was at 1 p.m. every week, without fail. My grandmother Theresa taught us that the food we ate was like medicine for the body, and if there were any arguments during eating, the food would turn to poison in our bodies. There were never any arguments. I passed this on to my children, and we always had fun at our meals.

As a child, food was symbolic of the love my family had for me. Family meals were an emotional experience for each one of us, especially for me. Being a Catholic, I cannot help but draw the comparison to receiving communion. Mealtime was a communion of the family, and our food was sacred because it was the medium of that communion.

"Deirdre, hang up your coat," my dad would tell me as we entered the Prairie Avenue house.

I would hang my coat on one of the lower coat hooks on the wall in the entry and run down the long hall into the dining room. The table would already be set, a chair for everyone. My grandmother Theresa used everyday dishes, which didn't match—but they were clean. She placed all the utensils on the same side of the plate, and I would not find out until later in life that that was not proper. It worked for us. And she would set a telephone book on my chair so I could reach my plate.

I would turn right from the dining room into the kitchen, where Grandma and Aunt Maffie boiled water for the macaroni and took the meatballs from the oven. They would both be sweating and wiping their faces (no air conditioning in those days), but would smile when they saw me.

"Buongiorno, Deirdre," Grandma would say.

"Buongiorno, Grandmacita."

Grandma would usually urge me to take a meatball or some other treat. "Mangia, Deirdre."

"Grazie, Grandmacita."

Grandma always wore a dress, a nice dress, covered with an apron. She wore her hair pulled back into a bun. Aunt Maffie also dressed well and wore her hair up on her head, wrapped up over something we called a "rat" and held in place with hairpins. That hairstyle always fascinated me. Every hair was perfect, and you could not see the pins.

Aunt Maffie would lean in, squeeze my cheek and murmur, "Mannaggia." Believe me, she squeezed hard. Then she'd say, "Get yourself something to drink."

My dad poured himself a glass of scotch, and I would have a root beer.

"Deirdre, go check the table and see if the spoons and forks are there," Aunt Maffie might say.

I always had some assignment, like helping mix the salad dressing or making sure all the silverware was on the table. Sometimes I would go with my grandmother upstairs when she wanted some wine or anisette, which she made herself. She would open the door to a locked room to reveal shelves filled with all kinds of liquor and stacks of cash.

All the cooking took place downstairs, with the whole family gathered around and milling through the rooms. The heavenly aroma of Theresa's meals would fill the whole house, just about melting our noses, it smelled that good. Like so many families at that time, most of the ingredients for the meals were fresh or had been canned the previous fall. The basement was filled with canned tomatoes, pickled eggs, olive oil, and many other condiments.

Occasionally, Grandmacita would send me out to pick up the meats she needed. One Saturday morning she sent me to the butcher shop and, when I returned home, she looked at the meats and sent me back to the store saying I didn't buy the right ones. When I told the butcher, "My grandma says that this is not the right meat," he stared down at me and answered, "Oh yeah, and who is your grandma?"

When I told him "Mrs. Capone" his faced immediately paled. "She is right. Please tell her I am terribly sorry." He sent me back to her with the correct meats. Grandma just smiled.

As Grandma cooked, I could hear the radio in the dining room broadcasting classical Italian operas. Sometimes she sang along. Uncle Al loved the opera; his favorite was Aida. Everyone in my family loved the opera and they encouraged me to study singing, which I did.

Uncle Matty, Aunt Annette, and Cousin Gabey, their son, would arrive and hang their coats on the wall hooks while my uncle Matty hung his hat on the hat rack in the living room. Like us, they all dressed in their Sunday best.

"Buongiorno, Mamacita."

Uncle Matty was the shortest and stockiest of my uncles. I remember he drank way too much, and he would sweat a lot. To me, he was the different one. His wife, Annette, was Sicilian, which didn't sit well with Aunt Maffie. Their son, Gabey, who was eight years older than I, was very handsome.

When they got themselves something to drink, Uncle Matty liked the dago red wine, while Aunt Annette would drink only root beer. But Gabey also drank wine and would let me take a sip, sometimes even more.

Usually arriving next were Uncle Bites and Aunt Larry. Aunt Larry (Loraine) was beautiful, with long blond hair and a striking figure. I remember wondering if I would ever be beautiful like her. As I mentioned in the previous chapter, their adopted son, Albert Robert, or Bobby, was my half brother. No wonder we looked so much alike—down to the beauty marks above our upper lips. Aunt Larry and Uncle Bites eventually divorced, and over the course of time, he went on to have many women in his life, all of them beautiful.

Entering next would be Uncle Mimi and his wife, Aunt Mary. Then came my grandfather Ralph. My father wanted me to call him "Grandpa," but Ralph really worked with me not to. In fact, he would put a bill in my hand each time I called him Ralph. He would come to Sunday dinners with his second and last wife, Val, but my Grandmother had us all understood tacitly that she was not family.

Finally, Uncle Al would arrive with Aunt Mae, the signal that the day had begun. His bodyguards would remain outside, but Grandma always brought food out to them after we had finished our dinner.

Uncle Al was just like all his brothers. He would go into the kitchen, give Grandma a kiss, call her "Mamacita," and of course squeeze my cheek, hard.

I think that Uncle Al was my grandma's favorite. She beamed when he came into her kitchen. She stopped whatever she was doing to give him a big hug and kiss. She squeezed his cheek. She didn't hug any of the others; they kissed her on the cheek, and she would continue cooking.

Aunt Maffie hugged and kissed Al, too. My, how she loved him.

When her sons greeted Theresa, they would often exchange words in Italian. She spoke English, but most of the time it was sprinkled with Italian. I was able to understand everything she said.

All her boys wore starched cotton, or silk, shirts and custom-made suits. I remember looking at their cufflinks and the stickpins in their ties. Their shoes were shiny. Grandma expected them to look their best. Each one of my aunts wore beautiful clothes, jewelry, and furs.

The men would disappear into the parlor shortly after arriving to talk business, my grandfather carrying a couple of ledger books with him. The girls would remain separate, bustling around the kitchen and sharing everything that had happened during the week. Oh my goodness, what gossip they would tell!

When it was time to eat, everyone took a place around the dining room table except Grandma and Aunt Maffie, who stayed in the kitchen. We began each meal with Uncle Al holding up his small glass of wine and saying, "Salute per cento anno," in his deep, raspy voice.

We would all hold up our glasses in turn and say, "Salute."

Most of them would then swallow the wine with one gulp.

After the toast, we ate. First came the antipasto. All the men would stand up and reach with their forks and stab what they wanted and put it on the first plate. Next was the soup, and we passed around the wine bottle in the basket. If it was pasta e fagioli, my grandmother would put a pot of soup and a bowl of pasta on the table. We would put some pasta in our bowls and ladle soup on top.

The wine bottle in the basket was passed around again.

Next course was the macaroni—our general word for pasta—served in a bowl with Grandmacita's gravy on top. If the pasta was spaghetti, the noodles were extraordinarily long. In those days, spaghetti came in very long boxes, and each noodle would be twice as long as the box. You don't see spaghetti that long anymore. I guess shelf space is too valuable.

We never cut the spaghetti into smaller pieces. I was taught very young how to use the larger spoon and swirl the spaghetti on my fork into a ball. Usually that took too long, and I wound up putting one strand in my mouth and slurping it through closed lips. The sauce flew everywhere, especially on me. After this course, I was usually full because I had eaten so many meatballs, but everyone else stayed in their chairs and talked and drank more wine—a lot more food was still to come.

The main course changed each week, and there would be special meats for various holidays, but usually it was meat, potatoes, and vegetables. Then the salad, that was always last. Grandma believed that eating the salad last would help us digest the rest of the meal. The first time I visited Italy I laughed when the salad was served after the main course.

After dinner—which usually lasted three hours—I would help Aunt Maffie clear the table and bring the dishes to the kitchen, where Grandma scraped the plates into the garbage can and filled the sink with hot soapy water. Very little food remained on any plates because Grandma regularly reminded us of the starving children in Europe. I could never figure out how cleaning my plate helped those starving children, but I did as I was told. As we cleared the table of dishes, Grandma placed big baskets of fruit and nuts on the table, which I loved.

After dinner, the boys took off their coats and ties, rolled up their sleeves, and lit up cigars—big fat Cuban ones. They chewed on the ends and blew perfectly round smoke rings, which always fascinated me. And they played cards, usually poker but occasionally an Italian form of blackjack called "Seven and a Half." During the game, they only spoke Italian. I think they did it because they swore a lot and didn't want me to understand.

I would be invited to sit on one of their laps to bring them luck. When my dad was there, I wanted him to win. When he wasn't there, I took turns rooting for Grandpa Ralph and Uncle Al. If one of them won, he would put some of the bills in my hands and tell me to put them in my pocket.

I later learned that Al used to be the top player, but regressed after his prison stay. It didn't stop him from loving to gamble, though. The Capone boys would bet on anything. In fact, Al and Ralph even placed bets on my birthday when my mother was pregnant with me.

I enjoyed seeing all the money in the middle of the table. Tens, twenties, and hundreds crumpled up and piled high about two feet long and two feet wide. I remember trying to count the money on the table but it was too hard because the stack kept changing. If someone ran out of money, he went home.

They were usually very serious and intent on winning, but I also sensed a feeling of camaraderie. Frequent smiles and bursts of laughter filled the room as they regularly teased each other.

I remember Uncle Al turning to Bites, who had a habit of mixing metaphors, and asking, "Hey, Bites. You still seein' that redhead?"

"Nah, I dropped her."

"How come?"

"Ah, she drinks like a chimney."

The room exploded with laughter. Uncle Mimi, who was drinking water, sprayed it across the table all over Uncle Matty and started coughing and laughing at the same time.

Then Grandpa Ralph said, "Yeah, and she smokes like a fish."

Another explosion of laughter. I was laughing too, though I wasn't quite sure what was so funny. Many years later when I watched Johnny Carson on the Tonight show spraying water when Ed McMahon said, "The King Lives!" it took me back to that card game and the most uproarious laughter I ever heard.

Then, as quickly as it started, the laughter stopped, and Al said, "C'mon, Matty, check or bet."

Sometimes I'd wander away from the card game and into the kitchen to join the women. I remember once finding them in a heated a debate on who was the best singer, Frank Sinatra or Bing Crosby. Maffie liked Sinatra and thought he was "cute and sexy." Aunt Mae and Aunt Annette said Crosby had the better voice, and they loved him in the "Road" movies with Bob Hope.

Maffie turned to Grandma, still washing the dishes, and asked, "Mamacita what do you think? Who's the best?"

Grandma just smiled and answered, "Opera, Caruso. That's music."

All agreed, but Maffie said, "Yeah, Ma, but we're talkin' about popular music, not classical."

Grandma said, "Well, opera is popular with me."

Usually long before the poker game ended, I fell asleep on the sofa in the parlor. My dad would wake me up at some point, and we would walk home together.

13

The End of the Al Capone Era
Miami and Chicago, 1947

I don't want to end up in the gutter punctured by machine gun slugs.
- Al Capone

The historians have it all wrong. My uncle Al did not die on Saturday evening, January 25, 1947 with his family at his bedside; and his funeral was not the sorry, lonely affair it's been made out to be. He didn't even die of complications of syphilis, as is commonly accepted.

Christmas 1946 is still fixed in my mind, as if the excitement and splendor of that year were enough to last a lifetime. The war had been over for more than a year, enough time for grown-up talk to turn away from death, Nazis, and faraway places, and turn toward celebration and family. Best of all, Uncle Al and Aunt Mae were coming to Chicago to spend Christmas with us. We were a family again, which meant spending time with my dad, whom I hadn't seen since Thanksgiving.

Any visit to 7244 Prairie Avenue was a welcome relief from the dour environment inside the tiny apartment where I lived with my maternal grandparents. Any visit with Al there made it positively electric. Everyone wanted to be near Al, and when he and Mae came to stay in the upstairs apartment, I knew there would be more food, more wine, more cash at the card games, and almost more excitement than a seven-year-old could stand.

Almost, but not quite.

I arrived at the Prairie Avenue house and the Christmas tree immediately grabbed my attention, positioned in the corner where the hat rack usually stood. It was hard to miss, because someone had decorated it not only with real, glowing candles and the usual ornaments, but also with thousand-dollar United States savings bonds. The money flowed when Al was around. He may have successfully hidden his assets from the federal government, but he never hid them from his family. The Outfit had their own retirement plan, and they took care of Al and his wife and son as long as they lived.

My dad took me into the living room where Uncle Al sat on a big chair in one corner. They started talking to each other in Italian, but I didn't care. It was music to my ears. I ran right over to Uncle Al and climbed onto his lap. He gave me a big hug. He had a very large neck and his skin always seemed moist. He smelled like scotch, and I noticed a glass on the side table. It was a familiar smell; both my parents drank scotch every day of their lives.

On his lap, I couldn't help but notice the big scar on his left cheek.

"Does it hurt?" I asked him. He just laughed.

When Uncle Al was just with family, he often acted silly, loving to make us all laugh. At times he seemed like a little boy. But as soon as an old friend entered the room, or someone from the Outfit came in, he would sit up straight, take on a very stern look, and a wide-eyed stare would come into his eyes. To me as a little girl, it was like watching someone put on makeup.

That Christmas, Uncle Al wore a white shirt, cufflinks that sparkled, and a tie held in place with a stick pin in the form of a woman's face. After Al's death, his mother had that cameo made into a charm that she wore around her neck. After Theresa died, Aunt Maffie gave it to me. When I wear it today, everyone comments on it.

When Uncle Al was with us, everyone in the family dressed in their finest clothes. Grandma would give my father money to buy me something new. I loved that. Very seldom did I have the chance to wear new clothes, even new shoes. In my own world, I was an outcast, and a poor outcast at that. In the special world of Prairie Avenue, I was a princess.

As soon as Theresa and Maffie said the word, we all went to the dining room and sat down together. Aunt Maffie put a thick Chicago telephone book on a chair for me. We ate and ate and ate, and drank wine, dago red. I toasted with wine with the adults, but after one glass, I had to switch to root beer.

This was the last time we would all be together, and when I close my eyes, I can remember every minute. Most of all I hear the noise, a low rumble that rose and fell as the conversation became more or less boisterous. The food and alcohol flowed, and the rowdy Capone boys jostled each other still, even as adults. But we all focused on Al, sitting at the head of the table, our eyes on him as if he were at home plate and we were the spectators.

After Christmas, just before the first of the year, Al and Mae returned to Florida. Uncle Al's 47th birthday was January 18, and Mae had a party arranged for him at their home on the Saturday before. All the high society people in Miami were invited.

Not long after the party, we got word that Al had become very ill. Aunt Mae arranged for two male nurses to take care of him around the clock. The doctors said that he had a mini-stoke, followed by a bad case of pneumonia. With his weakened immune system, the prognosis was grim. He had a couple of days at best, the doctors told us. My father, Grandfather Ralph, Grandmother Theresa, Uncles Mimi and Bites, and I took the train down to Miami, expecting the worst.

I can remember all the people in the house holding vigil. Uncle Al laid in bed, his eyes closed and his breathing labored. Aunt Mae called in their priest, and he offered prayers. My grandmother cried and prayed the rosary. Reporters with their cameras had gathered at the front gate. My grandfather asked them to leave us alone but they wouldn't, so he finally took some beer out to them. To my family, liquor solved everything.

After a few days, Uncle Al unexpectedly recovered. He could get out of bed and walk around, and even started playing cards again. He loved to play gin rummy. He started sitting at the card table on the pool deck and begged people to play with him.

Sure that Al was on the mend, my father decided we would return to Chicago where I already missed a few days of the second grade. My grandmother and Aunt Maffie returned a few days later. Uncle Al continued to improve and according to my aunt Mae, he was his old self again. My grandfather Ralph stayed in Florida to help Mae and to take care of financial matters.

On the morning of January 25, my seventh birthday, Al's doctor said he was well enough to go into the pool and swim some laps. Uncle Al was a strong swimmer, like my dad. After his swim, he took a shower with the help of his two male nurses. He got out of the shower, and the nurses prepared to powder his skin with talcum powder. In those days, the men in our Italian family always smelled of talcum powder. I can still recall that sweet smell. As Uncle Al stepped out of the shower, he dropped to the floor, dead in an instant from a massive stroke.

Suddenly, and without warning, the Al Capone Era came to an end. It was an era that saw him rise from obscurity and poverty in Brooklyn to become one of the most famous men of the twentieth century.

No doubt many Americans greeted his death with an emphatic "Good riddance." Many held the opinion that Uncle Al gave Italians a bad image of lawlessness and brutality. But the fact remains that when Al was growing up, Italians were the lowest on the totem pole of America's unofficial caste system. And although he did help to perpetuate the image of Italians as criminals, I believe that to a large percentage of Italians, Uncle Al engendered a sense of pride that one of their own could be considered the boss of Chicago, with most of the high-ranking police and politicians on his payroll..

As for his family and friends, his death was greeted with profound sadness. Gone was this man who had lifted the entire family from poverty to prosperity. Gone for Theresa was the loving son who at the peak of his reign as "King of Chicago" had phoned his mother every day. Gone was the generous man who took care of his brothers and sister financially and otherwise. Gone was my favorite uncle who bounced me on his knee, told me knock-knock jokes, taught me to swim, to play "rock, paper, scissors," and to play songs on the mandolin. He was so kind and gentle with me and the rest of his family. I couldn't believe it when I later learned of his title as "Public Enemy Number One."

The family knew of his plans to get out of the rackets once and for all and prove he could be successful in legitimate business. Call us naïve, but each member of our family always believed that Al never intentionally hurt an innocent person, though he did deal harshly with those who threatened him and his beloved family. Al himself swore, "I never stuck up a man in my life. Neither did any of my agents ever rob anybody or burglarize any homes while they worked for me. They might have pulled plenty of jobs before they came to me or after they left me, but not while they were in my Outfit."

Our family also knew of his struggles with syphilis, and they knew of his frequent bad dreams, reliving the trauma of the many attempts on his life. Over the years he dodged hundreds, if not thousands, of bullets. He learned of some plots that included bombs and others that involved poison. And he lived through a stabbing and the torture in Alcatraz.

He survived it all. But, this stroke brought it all to an end.

Or was it the end? The Al Capone Era seems to be constantly revived by the endless stream of books, movies, and television shows that either deals directly with Uncle Al or yields a strong influence by him, such as *The Godfather*, *The Untouchables*, and *The Sopranos*.

There are few people in the world, living or dead, with a name as well known as Al Capone. We know this from research, and from personal experience. My husband and I have visited more than 50 countries, and if we happen to mention to the natives that we are from Chicago, people often say, without knowing that I am a Capone, "Chicago. . . Ah, Al Capone!" (Sometimes this is followed by "Bang, Bang!!" as they mimic shooting a gun.)

On January 25, 2007, the sixtieth anniversary of his death, five hundred newspapers ran articles about Al Capone. The Associated Press ran a story that was picked up around the globe. Among its points: today, the Capone name is still synonymous with Chicago, despite city efforts to end or downplay the association; thousands of tourists every week take regular bus tours to Chicago spots that Capone made famous, including his burial plot, where many leave flowers and other tokens of respect; the Chicago History Museum records 50,000 hits every month for the portion of its Web site devoted to Capone; those fascinated with Capone include a large number of Europeans and other non-Americans who visit the city.

In just the two weeks prior to writing this paragraph, the following has transpired:

- The Wall Street Journal and many other newspapers in the United States and other countries, ran front page stories about uncle Al and our family.
- I have had several requests for interviews on national television and radio.
- Film makers have inquired about the documentary and screen play rights to *Uncle Al Capone.*

It appears that Uncle Al will forever be a part of American history and folklore.

———

On the day he died, one of Uncle Al's nurses called downstairs to Aunt Mae. When she saw his motionless body, she gasped but didn't say a word. Tears flowed down her cheeks, and she dropped to her knees and gently touched his arm. She leaned over and said something, barely audible, kissing him on the forehead. After a moment, she stood up, stiffened her body, and said, "We've got to call Ralph and Sonny." My grandfather had returned to his hotel the night before, thinking that all was well.

My grandfather immediately called Lou Rago, a good friend of the family and the owner of three funeral homes, Rago Brothers, in Chicago. Lou Rago made all the arrangements in consultation with my grandfather. In order to avoid arousing suspicion from the crowd of reporters that perpetually staked out Al's home hoping to get a photo of Al or Mae, Philbrick Funeral Home spirited Al's body away in a regular car. Lou Rago and his brother took turns driving back to Chicago on Highway 41.

My family wanted to bury Al with dignity and that meant they had to fool the press. That evening, my grandfather came out of the house and announced to the reporters that Al had died. Shortly afterwards, a hearse pulled up in front of the house and entered through the gate, which then closed behind it. A short while later, the gate opened and the hearse drove away with reporters following it, to Philbrick, where the next day a wake was held with a closed, empty casket. It was attended by family members who were still in Miami and a host of big shots from Florida, including Desi Arnaz, who had gone to St. Patrick's High School with Sonny. Two days later, the family returned to Chicago by train. Philbrick Funeral Home placed the empty coffin on the same train. The press reported that Al's body was on the train with them, but in fact it was already in Chicago, at Rago Funeral Home. In the meantime, the Outfit was putting out the word of when and where the real wake would be held, along with the day of the funeral mass and procession.

Uncle Al had a wonderful wake. I still remember how he looked in his coffin. It was a bronze color with a large cross on the inside of the lid. The handles were gold. The bottom of the casket was covered with a blanket of gardenias. There were so many flowers that they filled the other chapels and the lobby. After the wake, my family donated most of them to local hospitals—the funeral home did not have enough flower cars to take them to the cemetery.

I remember all the people. It was non-stop for twenty-four hours.

Mae had announced to the press that a private funeral would be held for Uncle Al on February 4, at Mt. Olivet Cemetery, but on the first of February, again unbeknownst to reporters, family and friends attended a high mass at Holy Name Cathedral, followed by a procession to the cemetery. The church filled with people and the procession lasted for several long hours. I was in the second car, sitting with my grandfather Ralph and my dad. Looking out the back window at the long line of cars, I couldn't even see the end of it.

The funeral procession ended at Mt. Olivet where Al was interred in a temporary grave in a vault in a wall.

Four days later, on February 4, a dreary, cold day, a Rago hearse took his coffin from the wall and transported it to the gravesite where a few members of the family, Grandmother Theresa, Aunt Mae, Grandfather Ralph, and Uncle Matty waited with a large number of reporters. The gravediggers served as pallbearers.

I can still remember Aunt Maffie returning to the Prairie Avenue house where I waited with my dad. She was very proud of herself. She said, "Well, we pulled it off!"

14

One Last Lesson
Chicago 1947 – 1950

All I ever did was sell beer and whiskey to our best people. All I ever did was supply a demand that was pretty popular. Why, the very guys that make my trade good are the ones that yell the loudest about me. Some of the leading judges use the stuff.
- Al Capone

1947 became a memorable year for many different reasons. Peace again filled the world. The Marshall Plan offered help to European nations so they could recover economically after World War II. Jackie Robinson became the first black major league baseball player. Al Capone died. And for me, I made my First Communion.

In the life of a Roman Catholic, the First Holy Communion is a very special day, and mine was even more important for my family, because it occurred less than four months after my uncle Al died. It gave everyone in my family something happy to look forward to.

Sunday, May 11, 1947, Mother's Day, was a gorgeous spring day, with just enough nip in the air to remind us that Chicago winters tend to linger. I must have been the happiest seven-year-old girl in Chicago. Grandma Theresa bought me a beautiful new dress with a matching veil, white patent leather shoes, and, of course, a purse. Waiting with the other second grade children to file into the St. Philip Neri Church, I felt like a princess. I was walking on air and nothing could bring me down—except maybe the nun who yelled at some of us girls for wearing the patent leather shoes.

"Look. Look in the shoe's reflection. Right up the dress! And in Church! I should make you all walk barefoot!"

But still, I was so excited. I was at the center of attention for the extended Capone family. Everyone showed up: Grandma Theresa, Al's son Sonny with his two oldest daughters, both my parents, my grandfather

Ralph, and my cousin Gabey. And everyone met at Grandma's afterward for a picnic prepared in my honor.

Grandmother Theresa, Deirdre Marie & Dennis outside church

The next day, however, wasn't so wonderful. To all my classmates in school, I had always been known as Deirdre Gabriel. No one knew my connection to Al Capone. But the South Shore edition of the *Tribune* outed me. In listing those who had received Communion, it added gratuitously, "Deirdre Capone, otherwise known as Deirdre Gabriel, made her First Communion at St. Philip Neri Church, with Al Capone's family in attendance."

Overnight, my entire second grade class stopped talking to me. I was shunned and I'd never felt so alone. A couple of weeks later, all my classmates were invited to a girl's birthday party at the South Shore Country Club—every boy and girl, that is, except me. I was devastated and overcome by the unfairness of it all. I didn't understand it then, but this would become a regular pattern in my life, a little girl made to pay for the sins of her elders.

The nun who taught our class—not the one who chastised me about the shoes—felt so sorry for me that she had a party just for me on the last day of school. I found out later that she had been one of my father's teachers when he attended school at St. Columbanus School on 71st Street. It didn't work to change anyone's mind about me. These children were simply not allowed to play with me.

Deirdre 'Gabriel' 2nd row, far right

Not until the sixth grade, four endless years later, when Barbara Werntz transferred to St. Philip Neri from another Catholic elementary school, did I finally make a real friend. By then, I guess, whispers of my real last name had subsided. Barbara and I remain friends today.

Next to the elementary school at St. Philip's stood an all girls high school, named Aquinas Dominican. There, I finally was able to escape the Capone legacy. I attended that school along with many other girls from St. Philip's, who continued to shun me, but there were also girls there from other elementary schools, and I made friends with them. To my second grade classmates, however, I was forever "that Capone." The sins of the father lasted a very long time.

———

Even at only ten years old, when the telephone's ringing startled all of us awake, I was overwhelmed by the sense that no good could come of it. Now, nearly sixty years later, I know that a late night phone call generally bears ill tidings of great sorrow. Good news has the patience and the good sense to wait for a decent hour. Bad news is rudely impatient.

On the morning of November 10, 1950, the phone set off an adrenaline buzz that worked its way up from my bladder to my brain in an instant. The apartment was dark, and though I'd shot upright before the echo of the first ring had stilled, my grandmother Marie Barsaloux and my grandfather Paul Barsaloux still lay sleeping, their chests rising and falling in peaceful slumber. Knowing that my grandfather was ill, I clambered over him, figuring that his sick sleep was less likely to be unsettled than my grandmother's. Only when my feet left the living room rug and hit the hardwood floor did it register how cold it was in the apartment. I ran down the long hallway to the phone nook, tugging my flannel nightdress up to my mouth to keep the chill from overwhelming me. I could feel my gooseflesh rising from my feet up my legs and spreading across my chest, as much caused by distress as the room's chill air.

In the near dark, I made out a shadowy figure coming from the opposite end of the apartment. I knew that my mother would be the only one in the household besides me who'd be awakened by the phone. A bit of a night owl, she probably had just drifted off into a light doze. As we approached one another, I was overwhelmed by a single thought.

"Mother, don't answer that phone."

By the time those words had torn their way past vocal chords as taught and tangled as wire, my mother had already put her hand on the phone.

"What are you talking about?" she half-whispered and half-snarled.

"They're going to tell you that my father is dead."

My mother's face distorted into a kaleidoscope of confusion, disgust, and impatience. I tugged at her arm, but she twisted away from me. I let go of her silk pajamas and stood slump shouldered for the inevitable.

"Hello?"

My mother's agitation was evident and her smoker's late-night congestion added a note of roughness that she probably hadn't intended. From the living room, a weak light spilled across the floor and pooled just shy of our feet. I heard my grandmother asking, "Betty?"

My mother cupped the phone more tightly against her ear and shrugged her shoulder up to the other unoccupied ear. She was so contorted that I couldn't see her face.

"Oh, that's too bad. What will happen next?"

That morning when I first heard her speak those words, and to an even greater degree a few minutes later when I learned that my premonition was accurate, my mother's calm shattered my equilibrium. It was as if, instead of learning of her ex-husband's death by suicide, she'd just been informed that a dress she'd dropped off at a dry cleaner had a wine stain too stubborn to be removed. The night's party would go on, but she'd have to find something else to wear.

As she casually leaned against the wall, I tried to read her face, how she held her body, but it was as if my mother had transformed herself into inscrutable script, whose shape I could vaguely make out as something intended to communicate but which conveyed no sense to me, no matter how hard I tried to read it. When she set the phone down and turned to tell me that my father was dead, I felt something similar—that she was speaking to me in a language I did not know but whose emotional meaning somehow resonated within my core.

Hearing that he was dead didn't surprise me—I had sensed that was the case. My father wasn't ill; the last time I had seen him was only a few days before, but the knowing I experienced in those pre-dawn hours was as profound as anything else I had ever known to be true. My mother continued to speak to me, relating the very few things that Aunt Maffie told her. I had the sense that she was speaking to me from a place high above me, like she was a judge raised on a dais, and I was being declared guilty of the charge that I'd brought against myself.

My father hadn't merely died. I'd killed him.

My mother instructed me to go back to sleep, a pointless task, but ever the dutiful little girl, I obeyed. Everyone else, with the exception of my younger brother who was still asleep, convened in the kitchen. I sat on the recently vacated Pullman bed I shared with my maternal grandparents. The tangled bedclothes lay in a human-shaped clump. I smoothed my hand across them, feeling their warmth recede.

From the kitchen I heard the white noise of my family's voices, punctuated by the percolations of the coffee pot. In my mind's eye, I could see the brown liquid leaping up through the glass bulb in the lid, steady as a heartbeat.

The smell of the brewing reached my nostrils, and I was instantly back in my grandmother's house on Prairie Avenue. Though Uncle Al had been dead for a few years and the family had begun to fracture, one essential element of the Capone family's traditional ways had remained. Sunday dinner at Theresa Capone's house was served promptly at 1 p.m., and everyone was expected to attend.

That previous Sunday, my mother relented and allowed me to go. I hadn't been allowed to attend in nearly two months, and in that same span of time, I hadn't seen my father. I remember that I was torn. As much as I wanted to see my father and his family, I knew how much my mother disapproved of my devotion to him and to them. One of the reasons why I frequently felt that I shouldn't implore my mother too strongly about attending Capone family Sunday dinners was that I feared she would be able to see my sin-stained soul. Every night when I knelt alongside the bed, I prayed that I would be able to go and live with my father. He adored me, and I adored him.

Today, I can see why my mother finally conceded to my request and let me attend that Sunday dinner. Thanksgiving was only a few weeks away. She'd be able to make a better case for my not spending the holiday with my father's family if I had just spent a Sunday with them.

As my mother walked me over to Grandmacita's house, I could tell that her having to give in a bit stung her. The closer we got to Prairie Avenue, the quicker her pace, as if she was eager to get this distasteful errand over with. We walked up the front steps, opened the outside door and she rapped sharply at the massive oak door, telling me to behave and then strutting away, smacking her hands together to rid them of the dust of the Capones.

In my ten-year-old mind, my mother's instructions to "Behave yourself," meant one thing: I was to be polite but distant. I mustn't say or do anything that would indicate that I was anything less than thrilled to be living with her, that I was as happy and content as any child could possibly be to be living alongside five other people in a cramped five hundred-square-foot walk-up. I wasn't to tell anyone that because of not only my name but also our poverty, I was considered even more of an outsider in that tightly knit parish community. The worse thing I could do, in my mind, was simply to act pleased to see my father, to let him know how much I loved him and missed him. To do so, I thought, would be an act of betrayal against my mother, the kind of thing for which I'd been punished before. To be honest, I don't know if I felt any loyalty to my mother, but I do know that I feared her.

I walked into the Capone house on autopilot. Even though I'd been away for many weeks, I was comforted by the fact that nothing appeared to have changed in my absence. The house was still somewhat dimly-lit. Even though Al was gone and the rest of his original Outfit either disbanded or landed in prison (Paul "The Waiter" Ricca and Tony Accardo were now running things.), Theresa continued her habit of shrouding the first floor windows in heavy brocade draperies. Still, the house felt warm and welcoming, not mysterious. I'd spent some of the happiest hours of my life in that home.

I did not know as I made my way to the Capone family dining room, that the object of so many of my prayers would be waiting for me there— my father, Ralph Gabriel Capone. In the years since his untimely death at his own hand at the age of thirty-three, I have made it my mission to better understand why he took himself from my life. Though he was never able to achieve in his life all that he aspired to and all that his family expected (or perhaps demanded), he did accomplish one thing that made all the difference to me—he was a wonderful father who loved me, if not long then certainly very, very well.

That's why what I did next that Sunday afternoon made me believe for many years after his death that I had killed him. Instead of running up to him and throwing my arms around his neck and allowing him to envelope me in a life-and-love-affirming hug, I ignored him. Out of the corner of my eye, I saw him in three-quarter profile sitting in the dining room, idly rifling a deck of cards, a cigarette dangling out of one corner of his mouth, a glass of some amber liquid raised halfway to his lips. Our eyes met briefly, mine wide as saucers, his squinting past the smoke of his ash-tipped Herbert Tareyton. I have to imagine what happened next because my eyes flitted away from him. I imagine him sitting straight up in his seat, taking his glasses off and rubbing the twin kidney shaped indentations on either side of his nose, and sadly shaking his head.

I landed in the arms of my uncle Matty, who pulled me in and then pushed me back to arm's length and told me how wonderful I looked. He kissed both my cheeks, and with each pass alongside his head, the smell of his sweat and the beeswax from the Brylcreem that held his hair, nearly overpowered me. He called his wife Annette over, proclaiming that I was growing into a real beauty before pinching my cheek and laughing, his breath smelling of wine.

I greeted the rest of my uncle Al's siblings—my uncle Bites and his beautiful wife Larry. My cousin Delores came to greet me, as did Uncle Mimi and Aunt Mary. After I ran the gauntlet of kisses and squeezed cheeks, I went into the kitchen. As usual, Grandma Theresa and Aunt Maffie were both hard at work preparing the dinner in a sauna-like environment.

Before I could ask for something to drink, root beer for me and the very few other non-drinkers, Aunt Maffie and Grandmacita looked at me, disapproval dripping from their sweating brows. They each stopped what they were doing, wiped their hands on the aprons that covered their Sunday best dresses, and walked over to me, shaking their heads. Instead of the usual, "Buongiorno," they stood over me scowling.

Aunt Maffie wrapped her strong fingers around my biceps and shook me. "Don't you know who's sitting out there?"

"My dad?"

"Yes. Why don't you talk to him?"

"I was saving him for last." I stammered searching for the excuse, and heard the tell-tale quiver in my own voice.

The two women looked at one another, their eyebrows rising and their eyes rolling in unison. Grandmacita brought the crucifix of her rosary beads that were always in her hand to her lips and walked back to the pot she had been tending.

"Can't you see how hurt your father is? Can't you see how upset he is?" Aunt Maffie pointed toward the dining room with the spoon she'd been using to stir the gravy. A drop of red sauce fell to the checkerboard tile. I continued to stare at it, afraid to make contact with my aunt's accusing gaze.

She was telling me to do what every fiber of my being had wanted to do. Maffie released me from her grip, turned me around, and with a gentle push, nudged me toward the dining room. All thoughts of my mother's anger melted in the moist air of that kitchen. I ran toward my father and watched as his face lit up. I climbed into his lap and snuggled against his chest and neck. He kissed me, telling me how much he missed me.

For the next few minutes the world around me disappeared, and I immersed myself in my father's affection and attention. I filled him in on what was going on at school, recited for him all of the times-tables, up to seven. As I got to seven times eight, his eyes were as big as the bowls that had been set out for the first course, pasta e fagioli. When I succeeded in getting the next two calculations right, he clapped his hands and kissed the top of my head.

"I think you're ready now for Sette E Mezo," he announced triumphantly, scanning the room to make sure that everyone had heard.

"Seven and a Half? Really?"

"Here," my father handed me half of the playing cards. "Take out the face cards, the eights, nines, and tens. Put the rest over here." He tapped a spot on the lace tablecloth next to his wine glass.

For the next few minutes, he explained the rules of the game to me, an Italian version of blackjack. Every time I got the king of diamonds, the wildcard, my father would slap his forehead and scowl at me in mock indignation. "You're sure you've never played this before?"

We took a break and joined the rest of the family when Aunt Maffie carried out a plate of antipasto. My uncle Mimi stood and raised his glass. He looked at each of us in turn, then inhaled noisily and nodded, "Salute per cento anno." His high voice was so different from my uncle Al's deep, raspy staccato. There was a brief silence and then everyone said, "Salute," in return and downed the red wine. Though he was gone, Uncle Al's presence still loomed large over everyone.

As soon as the wine glasses met lace, the men's arms shot out toward the platter of antipasto. I knew enough to wait, but as my father leaned over to stab a slice of proscuitto and an artichoke heart, he whispered to me, "This is the one time it's not ladies first. When all your uncles are through, then it's your turn."

Throughout the rest of the meal, my father instructed me on the finer points of etiquette. When we'd each received a ladleful of broth on top of our pasta, my father told me how to eat it. He stressed that it was important for a lady, with heavy emphasis on the word lady, to not bring her mouth toward the bowl. Instead, a lady should bring the soup to her mouth. Later, when we were down to the last few ounces of soup, he showed me that the proper way to get the last bits was to carefully tilt the bowl away from oneself. He demonstrated for me and I followed suit.

During the interim between courses, he elaborated more on what it meant to be a lady. "Deirdre, I don't want you to be like your mother. She doesn't act like a lady at all. You need to have respect for yourself. You don't go around chasing men and discarding them like they're a bad card."

I nodded. Message received.

Though our family dinners generally lasted more than three hours, to me it seemed as if that last dinner with my father was over in an instant. He talked to me the entire time, instructing me more on the importance of getting an education, having respect for my elders and myself, how to not ever be too dependent on any man in my life. From my adult perspective I can see now how odd this behavior was, how strange that I was being given a crash course for a final exam that wasn't to be handed out until years later. I understood later that my father was saying goodbye to me.

When it came time for me to leave, he didn't walk me to the hallway. He suspected that my mother might be there. Instead he hugged and kissed me again at the table, told me again how much he missed me and wished that things were different.

When I stepped outside, my mother was standing and talking to one of the two bodyguards the family kept on, more out of loyalty to them than as a necessity. I stood next to my mother while she finished her cigarette and her conversation. She looked at me and said, "You stink of cigars."

15

The Sins of the Father
Chicago, 1950

I have read in the papers of bank cashiers being put in cars, with pistols stuck in their slats, and taken to the bank, where they had to open the vault for the fellow with the gun. It really looks like taking a drink is worse than robbing a bank. Maybe I'm wrong. Maybe it is.
- Al Capone

I spent the day of my father's death quietly at home. Though my mother had promised she would speak to me about the conversation she had with my aunt Maffie and fill me on whatever details she could, she did not. At some point in the early afternoon, she left the apartment, and I didn't see her until she returned after what would have normally been dinnertime. To pass the time and to try to quiet my mind, I listened to a few records. Given my mood, I chose to play Bing Crosby's "After You've Gone" several times in succession.

All I knew of my father's death was that the police had discovered his body. He was alone in his apartment on South Wrightwood. I also knew, even at the age of ten, that thirty-three was far too young to die.

I tried to cheer myself up with "On the Sunny Side of the Street," and "When Irish Eyes are Smiling," but I kept coming back to my first choice. Even though the tune had a kind of up-tempo jazz feel, the lyrics still pierced me. At the time, I had no way of knowing that one of the reasons my father committed suicide was because of a broken heart.

My parents divorced a number of years earlier, and my father had fallen on even harder times than the ones that marked their marriage. According to a coroner's testimony at an inquest my grandfather Ralph requested (in those days you simply needed to pay the $6 fee and the hearing would be held), he suspected foul play as my father's organs were "flooded with alcohol."

The most obvious indication of his unhappiness and ultimate despair was the suicide note he left behind. Described in a *Chicago Daily News* article as "barely legible," the note read, "Dear Jeanie. Jeanie my sweetheart. I love you. I love you. Jeanie only you I love. I'm gone." Only when I was a grown woman would I learn the circumstances of his tortured relationship with this woman.

Though I wanted to know everything at the time, of course, my family didn't think it appropriate for a little girl to know the various and somewhat sordid circumstances of her father's suicide. Today, I find it ironic that the newspapers covered my father's death and the subsequent inquest. In my mind, what my father was trying to escape for most of his all-too-brief adult life was the notoriety that came with being a Capone. I suspect that to be true both because of what I've been told by surviving family members over the years and what I experienced myself. It's a terrible thing to be ashamed of who you are and where you come from. At the time of his death, he had been working on a memoir he titled *The Sins of the Fathers*.

In one regard, my father did live up to expectations and did not fail. Despite leaving my brother and me at such a young age, in the years when he was with us, he was a spectacularly good father. I adored him. I still love him.

My father was the one who prepared my meals, taught me to read, instructed me in how to conduct myself, and provided me with the kind of encouragement and support that, in the 1940s, would have generally been considered the mother's role to give. I only have vague recollections of my earliest years, but those memories are always of my father and me. I remember sitting on his lap as he read to me from the Golden Books Series, stories like *Three Little Kittens*, *The Little Red Hen*, and *The Poky Little Puppy*. Because of the plot of the last of those, my father would often serve me rice or chocolate pudding, or our very favorite "Black Cows" for dessert.

I suppose that most children feel safe and protected with their parents, and perhaps it is just that I longed for that same sense of belonging for so many years after his death that I feel that I am twice or thrice blessed for having him for even such a short amount of time.

I know it may seem I have deified my father and demonized my mother. But I know my father was no saint; he was a deeply flawed human being and his suicide was the ultimate expression of that. I understand that some people could look at his decision to end his life and say that choice negated any of the good he might have done as a parent up to that point.

I can't judge my father so harshly for his actions. I also know that my mother was just as flawed, if not more so, than my father. In her mind, I'm sure, she was more sinned against than a sinner herself. Her choice to leave my father was as much an act of desperation, in her mind, as my father's choice to leave this earth. After all these years, and all the attempts my mother made to pass me off to one relative or another, after the six marriages that followed her first to my father, after all the histrionics and hurt, I can say that I did love my mother. I loved her in the way that only a child can, knowing that she was not the woman I hoped she'd be, but nevertheless grateful for the lessons she taught me about how *not* to be as a wife, a woman, and a mother myself.

Mostly though, I'm puzzled by their behavior. Almost sixty years removed from the events that lead up to my father's death, the devastation has diminished its hold on my day-to-day living, but it hasn't entirely relinquished its grip on my imagination. I don't know what forces loomed on my parents to shape them into the people they became. What knowledge I've gained about my father and mother has come to me sporadically over the years. The slow accumulation of that information and the insights I've gained from having lived my own life form a picture as flawed as they were. I understand and accept that.

In many ways, I see my parents as emblematic of an era. Tragedy. Boom. Bust. Recovery. They were like characters in an F. Scott Fitzgerald novel. My mother was the quintessential flapper from the 20s. Like the proverbial moth to the flame that Fitzgerald used to describe Daisy in *The Great Gatsby*, my mother was drawn to the light of my father's apparent wealth. That the spring that produced that wealth had a foul source was of no concern to her, and she drank from it greedily. When it dried up, she simply moved onto whatever could satisfy that thirst elsewhere.

My father, by contrast, was expected to be the torchbearer for the family. By his own admission, my grandfather Ralph was tough on his son. While he was glad to see that he led a country club life, he felt my father hadn't paid his dues. He thought my father needed to be tougher, to have at his disposal the skill set that he himself gained from both a youth lived on the mean streets and a life in the racketeering business. He wanted to shelter his son, and thought my father should have to do the things he had done to attain the level of success he did. I could never quite get my head around that until I had children of my own. It was as if I hoped that somehow, maybe by osmosis, they would gain the insights and learn the painful lessons I learned without actually having to suffer them in reality. I think this is something most parents wrestle with.

———

When my mother finally came home on that awful day in November of 1950, Aunt Maffie accompanied her. Aunt Maffie's eyes were red and swollen but, despite her grief, she remained stalwart. She let me know that we were all going to the funeral home to see my father. She wanted me to get dressed so that I would look pretty for him.

Together, we went into the bedroom where my clothes hung neatly with my mother's. She selected a dress for me, a simple black jersey knit one that she had bought for me a few months earlier from Marshall Field's. She'd bought it and a few other outfits along with some pairs of underwear and shoes. I'd come home from school to find a shopping bag waiting for me. Along with the clothes was a box of the store's famous Frango Mint chocolates. I'd always associated that dress with the sweet smell of those candies.

After I dressed, I went into the main living area of the apartment. The two women stood at opposite ends of the room, my mother leaning against the door, my aunt peering vacantly out the window. Both had on their coats and hats, veils pinned up. I knew we weren't going to church—I didn't feel that same sense of the familiar I did every Sunday morning—but there was something of the same seriousness in the atmosphere. Aunt Maffie handed me a hat, a pair of red wool mittens, and a patent leather purse that matched my shoes. I shrugged into my pea coat and followed them down the stairs.

My father's wake was held at the Rago Brothers' Funeral Home, as Al's had been three years before. When we pulled up to the building, I was surprised to see a large number of men waiting at the entrance. They swarmed Aunt Maffie's car.

"G-d- vultures," I heard Maffie swear under her breath. My aunt got out of the car, using her door as a shield. She then shouldered her way past a few of the men. They were reporters, and like a scene out of a Hollywood movie, they were pressing forward, flashbulbs popping, and the mass of them, some with notebooks at the ready, others with microphones, moved like fedora-ed amoeba.

A couple of men I didn't know came to our rescue and formed an alley for us to pass through. I heard men calling my name and asking how I felt. I could feel my stomach acids rising in my throat. I was torn apart by my father's death, frightened by what I was about to see and now attacked by strange men asking me how I felt.

I wanted to scream, and when a few of them broke through the human barricade that had formed, I started to swing my purse wildly at these awful men. I felt Aunt Maffie grab my hand, but I shook free of her and hurled my purse, wanting nothing more than to hurt someone, anyone, to make him or her understand some of the pain I felt. A moment later, I felt my aunt's hand on my forearm, and my feet moved more quickly to keep up with her as she half-dragged me past the gauntlet and into the building's vestibule. Only then did I see a few police officers standing at the doorway with their arms folded across their chests looking as bored as if they were standing on a quiet corner in the Loop on a Sunday morning beat.

My aunt and mother were nearly breathless, and we all stood there for a moment smoothing our hair and gathering ourselves for our entrance in the viewing room. I had no idea what to expect when two of the Rago Brothers' employees swung the door open for us and somberly nodded. Compared to outside and the vestibule of the building, the viewing room was a hot house. A riot of flowers was displayed throughout the room, the overwhelming odor of gardenias and peonies choking me. The room was dimly lit, and in the wavering candlelight, I saw row after row of formally clad men and women staring soberly at me. A phalanx of black armbands seemed to turn and follow me. I recognized just a few of the faces, but I recognized the expression everyone wore—pity at the poor young thing that'd lost her father.

Our footsteps were smothered by the thick carpeting, and except for the murmuring of a few whispered conversations, the only sounds in the room belonged to the sleepy organ and the rhythmic counterpoint of sobs from a line of elderly women. They sat in a row, a black mass of dripping lace and rosary beads that bobbed and nodded, and softly beat their bony chests as they swayed in their seats.

I had lost track of my mother. I'm sure she was feeling overwhelmed. She was, after all, in enemy territory, the woman who had divorced the man who'd taken his own life with a mix of booze and pills. The only details

I'd heard of my father's death were on the ride over when Aunt Maffie said something to my mother about my father being found in bed on his side and how all the blood had pooled and distended his body. Aunt Maffie caught my eye in the rear view mirror and fell silent.

I followed the eyes of the other mourners as they swung away from mine to examine their own hands or to look straight ahead. My aunt Maffie had her hand on my shoulder, and she gently guided me toward the front of the room. There, on a raised dais was a casket. It seemed to be as large as a rowboat, though its surface gave off a polished sheen in the candlelight and the fittings seemed to glow like gold. My legs felt wooden, and it was if my feet continually snagged on the carpet as we moved toward the casket that held my father's body. I could feel my aunt's hand tremble on my shoulder. I looked up at her and saw her bring both hands to her mouth as she stifled a sob.

I was too numb to cry, too new to this neighborhood of grieving that my family lived with for so many years. I saw the kneeler in front of the casket and took my place in front of my father's casket. I could barely see over the lip of the coffin and the velvet lining that pillowed around him.

His eyes were shut, of course, and I was struck by how much he seemed to be a wax facsimile of the man I adored. Yes, he had the same receding hairline and the prominent eyebrows, but the blandly dour expression was not one that I recognized. This was not my father, not the jovial animated face that lit up the last Fourth of July when he'd brought me sparklers and showed me how to trace the letters of the alphabet in fire against the night sky. These were not the same alert and attentive eyes that held my gaze as I told him about my latest adventures at school. These stilled, silent hands through which a rosary snaked against the bloodless powdery flesh, were not the ones that touched my face and smoothed my hair and told me that I was loved.

I knew enough to say a prayer and to cross myself before rising again. This time, I was the one who was trembling. If that man in the casket wasn't my father, then where was he? When would I see him again?

As I made my way toward a seat in the front row, I saw my grandfather come into the room. A tall man, at 6 foot 2 inches, the tallest of the Capones, Ralph seemed to have been physically diminished by his grief. Seeing a face that seemed to have melted like wax released in me all the sadness, anger, and fear I'd kept pent up. It came out of me in a torrent of shrieks and tears.

The next thing I remember, I was seated in an unfamiliar apartment. A woman I didn't know smiled at me, carrying a tray with a teapot and a platter of cannoli, biscotti, and other pastries. She set them down on the mahogany coffee table and took a seat in one of the chairs.

"My name is Mrs. Rago. Are you feeling any better?" She pushed a cup of tea toward me and tilted the tray to show all of the sweets arrayed there.

I took a few sips of tea and tried to figure out how I had gotten where I was. Mrs. Rago must have read my mind, "Your mother and aunt are downstairs. They said that you should wait for them here. It was awfully stuffy in there. I'm surprised more people aren't feeling as faint as you."

I focused on the food in front of me. I realized I hadn't eaten a thing all day. In ways large and small, literally and figuratively, I would be hungry for the rest of my life.

―――

The next day dawned clear, crisp, and cold. If it weren't for the fact that we were burying my father, it would have been a nice November day for Chicago.

After the high funeral mass at Resurrection Church, I rode in the family car in the funeral procession to the graveside service at Mt. Carmel Cemetery. At one point, my mother leaned her head against the window, and drew the backs of her gloved fingertips across the cool glass. To herself, but loud enough for me to hear her, she said, "Maybe there was something I could have done to help him."

I can recite for you the events that likely lead to my father's decision to kill himself, though I could never adequately describe what he felt. I do know a few things about my father's activities in the days between our last meeting at Sunday dinner and his death. He went to see Don Freund, his best friend, who had once introduced him to my mother. He was away, but he did get to visit briefly with his good friend's parents.

I also know that in the aftermath of my father's death, the neighbors in his apartment building made the usual statements about someone who fell victim to tragedy. He was a quiet man. Kept mostly to himself. He ate most of his meals in his apartment, heating up beans on the stove. Nothing revelatory or unique in that—simply the sad facts of a broken life.

He was clearly in love with Jeannie Kieran, a singer at a Rush Street club where my father worked part-time as a bartender. The management knew about my father's family associations, maybe even reveled in the knowledge of having a colorful character on staff, but they didn't like their girl singer hanging around a bartender. They told young Jeannie—she was twenty-one and my father thirty-three—that if she continued to insist on seeing my father, she'd lose her job. She was out of town the night my father drank himself to death. I don't know if she came to the wake or the funeral, or if she ever set foot on the grounds of Mt. Carmel cemetery where his body was interred.

I do know this. In the weeks preceding my father's suicide, a lawyer in Chicago by the name of Marvin Bas was murdered. Marvin Bas was dating Jeannie Kerin and he was upset with Jeannie after seeing her in a bar with my father. He was quoted as telling her "You'd better stick to the boys with the crew haircuts." A few days before his death, Mr. Bas had been approached by Bill Drury, an informant on the mob who offered his services to Senator Estes Kefauvers' who headed a special Senate committee investigating organized crime. Drury arranged a meeting with one of Kefauver's investigators promising to offer him entry into Chicago's scheming underworld. Word had it that Drury was also getting ready to channel embarrassing information about Police Captain Daniel A. "Tubbo" Gilbert, the Democratic candidate for Cook County sheriff, to Tubbo's Republican opponent. In his eighteen years as chief investigator for the state's attorney, Gilbert's investigators had never contributed any evidence that lead to the conviction of a single Chicago mobster.

Subsequently, Drury contacted his own lawyer, claiming he needed protection. They petitioned Senator Kefauver's office for assistance in the securing of bodyguards. The request came too late. Drury was gunned down as he backed his new Cadillac into his garage. A few hours later, Bas was gunned down in the streets beneath an L platform.

My father was hauled in for questioning in the murder investigation. That's how he discovered that Mr. Bas was also dating Jeanne Kieran. My father had fallen from grace and was now considered by some in the Chicago Police Department to be just one of the usual suspects to be rounded up as a matter of course. But he was never a part of the Outfit. He was destined for greater things until the sins of the fathers caught up to him.

I can't help but wonder if, in those last agonizing conscious moments of his life, as he gagged on the last of the Seconal and washed them down with Johnny Walker, he knew as I do, that those weren't the bitterest of the pills he'd been forced to swallow in his brief life.

The following story was published in the *American Weekly* following my father's funeral. It was written by W. T. Brennon

There are minor variations, but everywhere he tried to find work the story was almost the same.

"Name?"

"Ralph Capone."

Always the quizzical look. "Any relation of Al Capone?"

"Yes, a nephew."

"Sorry. There's nothing open."

After a while young Capone – Risky, his friends called him – gave up and changed his name. It was obvious that no Capone was going to find a legitimate job easily anywhere around Chicago.

His Father, Ralph Sr. proprietor of a resort at Mercer, Wis, had kept him in private schools since he was a boy and had carefully shielded him from any contacts with the underworld empire that his uncle Al had organized. Risky graduated from a prep school in Collegeville, Minn; attended Notre Dame two years and won a B.S. degree at De Paul University, later enrolling in Loyola Law School. Apparently he passed the bar but did not obtain his license.

There were all sorts of jobs where the name of Capone might have been an asset – jobs that were shady in spots, to be sure, but within the law and promising an alluring income for a young fellow just out of school. Risky didn't try for any of those. He was proud of his engineering degree and wanted to put it to use.

When no engineering firm displayed any interest in his services, he took the name of Ralph Gabriel and opened a plant in South Chicago to manufacture prefabricated homes. The business did well. He married, became the father of a girl and a boy and thought he was set for life.

The first bad break came when an employee of a construction firm stopped him on the street.

"Remember me?"

"No," Risky said. "I don't think I do."

"Well, I remember you." The man said. "We used to go to school together and your name isn't Gabriel."

The word got around. Before long a rumor spread that Capone, using another alias, was operating a gambling joint on the side. The police investigated and discovered the report was unfounded but by that time numerous customers had withdrawn their business. The plant had to close.

Risky changes his name again and opened a used-car lot. It flourished for a while – until his name caught up with him. "Did you ever know a Capone that wasn't running some kind of a racket?" people said. That was enough. The lot failed.

His wife lost confidence in him and divorced him, winning custody of the two children.

He tried many ventures after that, among them a briefly successful company for the manufacture of cigarette lighters. He tried many aliases too, but they didn't last long and neither did the businesses. Finally, almost broke, he became a bartender in a Chicago nightclub reverting once more to the name of Ralph Gabriel. Some of his customers knew who he was, but they didn't mind. It was hardly the job for which his education had prepared him, but he was happy t have achieved a comparative anonymity.

One of the attractions at the club was Jeanne Kerin, a 21 – year - old comedienne. She and Risky fell in love. Marvin J. Bass, an attorney who knew Jeanne, saw them together. Calling her to one side he said:

"You'd better stick to the boys with the crew haircuts, Jeanne. That fellow is Al Capone's nephew."

"Thanks, pal," Jeanne said. "It's sweet of you to advise me, but Risky told me who he was the second time we were out together. I'm happy and I don't think it's anybody else's concern."

It became the concern of a number of people, however, because of two murders.

Risky who had never been of a much of a drinker, began to drink heavily. When he failed to leave his apartment for 24 hours, the superintendent knocked and receiving and, receiving no response, called the police.

They found the 33 year old college graduate sprawled on the bed, dead. On the table was a half – empty bottle of whiskey beside an empty medicine vial, the label of which said the contents would be fatal if consumed with alcohol.

A scrawled unfinished note on the desk said: "Jeannie (sic), my sweetheart, I love you. I love you. Jeannie,(sic) only you I love. Only you. I'm gone…"

There was a difference of opinion as to what ended Ralph Capone's life. The official report said alcoholism. The police said, off the record, that he poisoned himself. One of the detectives may have come even closer to the truth.

"There lies a kid," he said, "who was destroyed by a name."

My grandfather was not sure that my father took his own life so he asked for an autopsy and an inquest.

The following are two death notices from the *Chicago Tribune.*

1950-11-12

Chicago Tribune (IL)

CAPONE

Edition: Chicago Tribune

Ralph Gabriel Capone, son of Ralph J. Capone, loving father of Deirdre and Dennis, beloved grandson of Theresa Capone, dear nephew of Mafalda. Funeral Monday, 8:15 a.m. at chapel, 624 N. Western avenue. Interment local cemetery. ARmitage 6-7800. Copyright 1950, Chicago Tribune. For permission to reprint, contact Chicago Tribune. Record Number: 19501112dn082

1950-11-14

Chicago Tribune (IL)

ONLY HIS FAMILY AT SERVICES FOR CAPONE NEPHEW

Edition: Chicago Tribune

Ralph Gabriel Capone Jr. was buried yesterday. Only family members attended services in Resurrection church, 5072 Jackson blvd. Burial was in Mount Carmel cemetery.

Capone, 33, was found dead in bed in his apartment at 656 Wrightwood av. last Thursday. Cause of death reportedly was alcoholism. An inquest was continued to Dec. 1 pending an examination of his vital organs.

Capone, the son of Ralph [Bottles] Capone, ex-gangland lieutenant, and nephew of Al [Scarface] Capone, tried to escape their notoriety. However, in March, 1948, he was placed on probation in Minneapolis for attempted

16

Life After Al and Dad
Chicago and Las Vegas, 1950 – 1963

People who respect nothing dread fear. It is upon fear, therefore, that I have built up my organization. But understand me correctly, please. Those who work with me are afraid of nothing. Those who work for me are kept faithful, not so much because of their pay as because they know what might be done with them if they broke faith."
- Al Capone

My father's suicide changed my life in the most negative way possible. I hated myself. I hated God. I was deeply depressed and wanted to die. I tried to a couple of times by taking too many aspirins, but then I forced myself to throw them up. I also walked out into Lake Michigan one night, wanting to walk until I could not touch the bottom and then sink, but I wasn't brave enough. I am happy today that I didn't, but my adolescence was miserable.

I responded to the depression by gaining weight and lots of it. By the time I was thirteen, I was 4 foot 10 inches tall and weighed close to 200 pounds.

Kids in elementary school can be cruel, and I was the brunt of some pretty cruel remarks. I was once told by a girlfriend, "I like having you around because next to you, I look good."

Before being admitted into the high school I wanted to attend, Aquinas Dominican, I had to be examined by a doctor. He was appalled by my weight gain—I remember him yelling at me. His solution was to prescribe Dexedrine. Sure enough, it worked. After taking the Dexedrine for a while, I looked great. I was slim, could eat anything I wanted, and I had tons of energy. When I began high school I wore a size 18; by senior year I wore a size 5 and had to hold my uniform skirt up with safety pins.

When I was sixteen years old, my aunt Maffie invited my mom, my brother Dennis, and me for Easter, along with Uncle Matty, his wife Annette, and their son Gabey. Maffie made lamb stew with boiled beets and, most importantly, her Easter bread. I always wanted to learn how to make it. She put whole eggs on top of the dough, braided additional dough on top of them, and then baked it. The eggs never split open or cracked. She asked me to arrive by 10 a.m. to learn how to braid the bread. While it was baking, she showed me how to make the lamb stew—and shared memories of Easter at Theresa's house with the Capone boys.

On the Easter table at Grandma's house was always a baked sheep's head in the middle of the table. My dad and his uncles fought because each one wanted the eyes, their favorite part. They shared the brain and tongue, but the eyes were heaven to them.

Grandma, too, would make an enormous loaf of Easter bread. She said the eggs baked in the dough represented a new life, which is what Jesus had attained by dying for our sins, and she taught me that Easter bread could only be made at Easter time. She believed that at other times of the year, the dough would not rise.

I had a great Easter dinner that year with Maffie, but I remember that the subject of the Dexedrine I was taking came up. Gabey got on my case about it and insisted I get off the stuff. Maffie agreed with him. But their argument fell on deaf ears because I was afraid of going back to being obese. It was a result of that drug use that I can remember very little of my teenage years.

After I graduated from high school, I received a full ride scholarship to the University of Miami, where my mother had briefly moved our family. But two weeks before I was to leave for school, my mother decided we should go back to Chicago and told me that I had to get a job, not go to school, and help pay for my brother's education. "Only boys should be educated," my mother said. "Girls get married." I realize today that she was imposing her own regrets about dropping out of high school on me.

We lived in a small, one-bedroom, one-bathroom apartment on the South Side of Chicago. My brother, who was fourteen, had to sleep in the living room on a sofa, and I had to share our one bed with my mother, but she loved that apartment because it was right on the beach and she could lay out in the sun and meet guys.

It was at this time in my life that the effects of my difficult childhood, the loss of my father, and the shame at being a Capone finally caught up with me—and nearly drowned me. I found a job at the insurance company, only to lose it six months later when my boss discovered my real name. In the wake of that painful experience, I began dating the man who would become my first husband. Though I told him I was Deirdre Gabriel, he discovered my real name through mutual friends of ours. The family connection suited him just fine—he wanted to be part of the mob, and that's why he was interested in me in the first place. But he also knew I was a good girl. He needed to find a way to control me—and he found it.

In 1958 he date-raped me. Then he told me that I was "damaged goods," and no other man would want me. A combination of my naivety, poor self image and Catholic education led me to believe him. Thinking I had no other recourse, and against my family's wishes, I started making plans to marry in July of 1959.

On April 20, my aunt Maffie phoned me at my new job. She said Aunt Mae was in town and they wanted me to come over after work. I went there expecting a lecture, especially from Aunt Mae, but instead after dinner Aunt Maffie handed me a spiral notebook. April 20, 1959 was the television debut of *The Untouchables*.

I found out that night that my aunts were suing Desilu Productions for $1 million—though I think the suit was more from heartbreak than financial gain.

Desi Arnaz's father had been a friend of Al and Ralph's. His father, Desi, was Mayor of Santiago and then served in the Cuban House of Representatives. My grandfather Ralph helped secure his release from prison when he was jailed after the 1933 Cuban revolution. Desi and his parents then fled to Miami early in 1934, where my aunt Mae helped them find a home and got Desi enrolled in Saint Patrick's Catholic High School, where Sonny was a student.

Ralph Capone and Desi Arnez Sr.

Desi and Sonny became very close friends and they got together every day at Al's house to sing and play the bongos together.

Sonny would also confide in Desi. They became close friends just when Al was being transferred to Alcatraz, and Sonny openly shared all his fears and pain. Aunt Mae told me that she thought their relationship was good for both of them. They both were only children, boys, and had fathers that had been in prison.

And now, in 1959, Desi was preparing to premier a television show that was surely based on the secrets Sonny had confided in him. Mae was hurt and furious, but Sonny was married with four children, owned a restaurant in Miami, and did not want the publicity. He told Mae that if she wanted to fight it, she and Maffie would have to do so on their own—and they did.

She begged Desi not to go forward with the show, but by that time, it was no longer in his hands. The choice belonged to Lucy—Lucille Ball, his wife and partner.

That evening at Maffie's house, my aunts asked me to write down the number of times I heard my uncle's name mentioned—as a record for their case. It was not mentioned once.

The second episode was on April 27, 1959. I again had to write down the number of times I heard the Capone name. Again, none. Lucy changed the focus from Capone to Nitti in those first two episodes. Maffie and Mae dropped the suit, but the hurt never went away. Sonny divorced and moved into hiding after that series.

Aunt Mae did try to talk me out of getting married, but I was afraid that if I told her the truth about why I had to marry, my whole family would disown me. So, I went ahead with it in July 1959. It wasn't until June 1961 that I was able to escape the control of my first husband, leaving with my daughter, only a year old, and my son in my belly. I cannot tell you how many times during those brief but endless two years the police were called because he literally tried to kill me.

I moved into my mother's studio apartment on the North Side of Chicago. In November of 1961, a Christmas card addressed to me at my mother's old address arrived in her mailbox. It was from Bob, a man whom I'd met at the life insurance company and with whom I'd had to break off my relationship fearing his rejection if he knew of my relations with my first husband. I called him, and—a miracle—we picked up our romance where we left it.

———

My marriage with Bob marked a new era in my life. I was still a Capone, but I was finally able to begin to feel centered and at peace with my identity. In a sense, being a Capone became secondary as I began to raise a family of my own—but over the years, there were still reminders of just how notorious my family was.

In 1963, Bob and I eloped and went to Las Vegas for our honeymoon. The day after our wedding I called Aunt Maffie with the news. She was very excited and happy for me. When I told her that we were going to a show that night to see Ella Fitzgerald and Joe E. Lewis, she said, "Joe E. Lewis? I knew him many years ago when he was working for Al in Chicago. I think he liked me. God, I haven't seen him in ages. Listen, give your waiter a note to give to him. Say that you're my niece. Include my phone number and ask him to call me the next time he's in Chicago."

I told her I would, but I forgot to do it at the show—probably because it was so terrific that I got absorbed. Mr. Lewis was a riot. He did his act with a glass of whiskey in his hand and most of his jokes had to do with drinking. I still remember some of his one-liners, the same jokes Frank Sinatra told when he played Joe E. in the movie *The Joker Is Wild*. My favorite was, "You're never too drunk if you can lie on the floor without holdin' on."

The next day, Bob and I walked into the Flamingo Hotel coffee shop for breakfast about 2 p.m.—remember, it was our honeymoon. As we were being seated, I accidentally bumped the hand of a man at the next table as he extended it to turn the page of his newspaper.

I quickly apologized—and realized the man was Mr. Lewis. When I saw who it was, without thinking, I said, "Oh, my aunt Maffie said to say hello."

With a puzzled look he said, "Your aunt, Maffie?"

I said, "Yes. Mafalda Capone."

"Mafalda?" He repeated, a look of surprise coming over his face. "Is she here?"

I said, "No, she's in Chicago, but she wants you to call her whenever you're in town."

"Hell, I haven't seen her in over twenty years. How is she? And you're her niece?"

"Yes, my maiden name is Deirdre Capone, but I just got married yesterday. This is my husband, Bob."

They shook hands, and Mr. Lewis insisted that we join him for breakfast. I guess he had stayed in bed late, too.

During our conversation, he revealed that he and Maffie once had a little flirtation going on, but nothing ever came of it. "For one thing, she was married, and I sure as hell didn't want to mess with Al's sister," he explained.

But he told us that though he feared Al, he came to regard him as a good friend. He pointed to the scars on his face and neck and said, "Most people think Al did this to me, but he didn't even know what happened 'til he read about it in the paper. Later he told me that if I had come to him with my problem with McGurn, he could have prevented it. And you know what? I'm sure he would have. But I didn't know it at the time. You live and learn."

Mr. Lewis explained the problem he had with Jack McGurn. Al had set McGurn up as part owner of the Green Mill, a very popular speakeasy on the North Side of Chicago. Joe E. Lewis, singer and comedian, was the Green Mill's biggest draw.

But they were only paying him $650 a week and a competing club, the Rendezvous, offered him $1,000 a week, so he decided to take the offer and leave the Green Mill when his contract was up.

But when he told McGurn he was leaving, McGurn said, "The hell you are. You'll stay at the Green Mill until I tell you to leave."

"It's a free country," Mr. Lewis answered.

"Not for you it isn't. You won't live to open at the Rendezvous."

Mr. Lewis told Bob and me, "I was scared, but I was also stubborn as hell...always have been. So I hired a bodyguard and started performing at the Rendezvous. After a week or so, everything seemed cool. So I fired the bodyguard, and a couple of days later McGurn and a couple of other guys I didn't recognize broke into my hotel room, cut me up, and left me for dead. But like I said, I'm stubborn, too stubborn to die. And here I am over thirty years later, still kickin'.

Actually, your uncle paid my medical expenses, and later gave me work and money whenever I needed it. He was unique. He had a big heart. He was a good guy to have as a friend, but a bad ass to have as an enemy.

As I got to know him better, I realized that he was an especially good friend to entertainers. He liked to associate with talented people, and entertainers were attracted to him. Not only was he more well-known than any performer on Broadway or in the movies, if you were his friend you were protected. Performers were routinely robbed and had money extorted from them. But the thugs would leave you alone if it became known that you were Al's friend."

After breakfast, Mr. Lewis picked up our tab, saying, "This one's on me. A little wedding gift from Joe E. And you tell your Aunt Mafalda I will call her the next time I'm in Chicago." His last words to us were, "Now you kids get on with your honeymoon and don't waste it talkin' to old farts like me."

17

"The Ant" Offers a Job

*I'm a business man. I've made my money supplying a popular demand. If
I break the law, my customers are as guilty as I am.*
- Al Capone

One last story.

After my uncle was jailed for tax evasion, Francesco Nitto, a.k.a. Frank "The
Enforcer" Nitti, assumed power of the "Outfit." My grandfather told me
that even though Nitti thought he was in control, as I mentioned before,
the real boss was Felice DeLucia, better known as Paul "The Waiter" Ricca.
Shortly before Uncle Al had his trouble with the IRS, a new organization
formed called the National Crime Syndicate. My grandfather told me that
after Uncle Al attended their first meeting in 1929, he made the decision
that it was time for his people to move on. He did not like the direction the
new syndicate favored. It was to be a loose affiliation of the major Italian
and Jewish crime bosses of the day, men such as Charlie "Lucky" Luciano,
Meyer Lansky, and, of course, my uncle Al. Its "enforcement arm" drew the
nickname "Murder, Inc."

While my uncle and grandfather were still in prison, Prohibition ended
and the Outfit moved into gambling, loan sharking, labor, and racketeering.
They also extended their operations into Milwaukee, Madison, Kansas City,
and even into Hollywood, where they attempted to run their extortion
tactics on the motion picture labor unions.

Nitti was accused of the extortion and refused to take the fall for the
Outfit. He committed suicide in 1943. After serving time in jail for tax
evasion years earlier, he decided to end his life rather than face jail again.
Paul Ricca then became the boss and Tony ("Joe Batters," "The Big Tuna")
Accardo was his enforcer. Later in 1943, Paul Ricca was convicted for his
role in the Outfit's plot to control Hollywood. He stood to serve ten years,

but magically only served three due to the Outfit's "fixer" Murray "The Camel" Humphreys. By the way, don't you love the nicknames?

Tony Accardo became the boss when Ricca was in prison, but when he was paroled, they placed a condition on his release that he could not associate with "mobsters." My grandfather said that Ricca did serve as a senior consultant to Accardo. He operated behind the scenes just as my grandfather had with his brother Al.

In 1956, my cousin Dolores Maritote married and I was a bridesmaid. All of the above mentioned people except Nitti were in attendance, along with Sam Giancana, who took over control of the Outfit in 1957. In the photo below, you will find all the above named people plus others of the day, but it is difficult to tell who is who. You will also find the African American athletes and entertainers that my family helped.

I never saw any of those individuals again until 1970 when Grandpa Ralph took Bob and me out to dinner at the *Ivanhoe* restaurant and night club in Chicago. It was a rare occasion. As we were being shown to our table, I heard a man say, "Ralph, what the hell are you doin' here? I thought you were up in Wisconsin."

Ralph glanced over to see who was speaking to him in this manner. A big grin sprang to his face and he responded, "Tony, what's up?" I turned to see who it was but didn't recognize the face right away.

Ralph said, "I came down for some business, nothin' big, and I'm taking my granddaughter and her husband to dinner. You remember Deirdre? This is her husband Bob. Kids, this is Tony Accardo. We go way back together." Tony shook hands with Bob and gave me a hug.

"Sure I remember Deirdre," Tony said warmly. "Honey, you're more beautiful than ever."

I felt myself blushing as I said, "Thank you."

Tony said, "Why don't you join us?" gesturing to the man next to him. "Oh, this is Anthony Stuart." We shook hands with Mr. Stuart as Tony kept insisting that we join them. "We've got plenty of room, and we're boring the hell out of each other" Tony added, "and I'll pick up the tab."

Bob said, "If it's OK with Ralph, it is OK with me." Ralph resisted a little, then acquiesced.

We ordered some drinks, and while Ralph and Tony began speaking to each other in Italian, Mr. Stuart, a short dark-haired man whom I guessed to be about thirty or thirty-five years old, asked if we were both from Chicago. Bob said yes, that I had grown up on the South Side and he grew up on the Northwest Side.

Mr. Stuart said, "Yeah? Where on the Northwest Side?"

When Bob said around Irving and Austin, Mr. Stuart asked, "Where'd ya go to school?"

"Steinmetz," Bob replied.

This information was greeted by Mr. Stuart with a big grin and a loud, "No shit! That's where I went, but I quit after two years. I figured I didn't need school to make money. The street was my school."

During dinner, Mr. Stuart and Bob took turns telling jokes and seemed to be enjoying themselves. He even complimented Bob on his suit. When Bob told him where he bought it, he said that he used to buy his clothes there, but switched to buying wholesale. "In fact I'm opening my own men's store at *Circus, Circus* in Las Vegas. I'll be looking for someone to manage it for me. Think you'd be interested?" Bob told him Vegas was fun to visit, but he wouldn't want to live there.

All through dinner Ralph and Tony drifted in and out of our conversations, but mostly had their own private gabfest going. While we were having dessert, I felt a foot gently rubbing against my leg. I knew it was Mr. Stuart's, so I moved my legs a few inches away from him, but in a little while I felt it again. Something about this man made the hair on the back of my neck stand on end. He was frightening. I excused myself to go to the ladies' room.

When we said our goodbyes and left the restaurant, Ralph grabbed Bob's arm and took him aside. Ralph knew that when Bob married me, he had kept his distance from the family, and had let it be known that he wanted nothing to do with the Outfit's business, and that was fine with Ralph. That was smart.

"Now keep being smart," Ralph said insistently. "Stay the hell away from 'The Ant.'"

"The Ant?" Bob asked, puzzled.

"That guy's name isn't Stuart," Ralph explained. "He's Tony 'The Ant' Spilotro. He's the meanest, craziest SOB I've ever seen. And that includes Jack McGurn and Hymie Weiss. He kills people just for the fun of it. And he likes to torture them first."

Bob naturally assured Ralph that he'd have nothing to do with Spilotro. He told Ralph that he recognized the name, and had heard some bad things about him.

"Guys like him scare the hell out of me," Bob said.

"There are no guys like him," Ralph replied. "He's the worst."

Bob assured Ralph that there was no way in hell he would ever have anything to do with Spilotro, or Accardo, or any of them.

Many years later in the movie *Casino* with Robert DeNiro and Sharon Stone, Joe Pesci played the role of Nicky Santoro, a character based on Tony Spilotro. In 1986, Spilotro was found buried with his brother Michael in an Indiana cornfield just southeast of Chicago. They had been badly beaten and evidently had been buried alive.

Good thing Bob didn't take that job in Vegas!

Epilogue

Al Capone: Not Guilty on All Counts
Chicago, Present Day

What do you want to do, get yourself killed before you are thirty?
You'd better get some sense while a few of us are left alive.
- Al Capone

In 1991 the American Bar Associations Litigation Section, following a practice they have often used, decided to retry the 1931 Capone income tax case. The Capone case was chosen because the ABA Annual Meeting was in Chicago.

This was an actual trial and not merely a reading from the original transcript. The lawyers were limited to the facts in the original transcript and newspaper articles and books related to the trial or the facts of that time.

The judge was Chicago Federal District Court Judge Prentice Marshall, an outstanding jurist who had been a successful litigation partner in a top Chicago law firm and later a distinguished professor of trial advocacy at the University of Illinois Law School. He was also a founder of and major contributor to the National Institute of Trial Advocacy.

The jurors were from the actual venire of jurors from the Northern District of Illinois. They were volunteers who were paid by the federal jury rate but were not told the nature of the case they were to hear. Actually there were sixteen in all and they all sat on the weekend case.

To say the least the program was well received by the American Bar Association lawyers and judges. Over 1500 attended the trial in the grand ballroom of the Palmer House Hotel.

Catherine Crier supplied the audience with background information before the start of the actual trial.

Department of the Treasury senior staff acted as the prosecution witnesses. The prosecutory were personally selected top trial lawyers from the Department of Justice. All told they all did a wonderful job.

I wish my uncle could have been represented by the two defense attorneys Terence MacCarthy and Mike Tigar who represented him in this retrial. The record shows that my uncle was represented by two attorneys who did a very poor job.

MacCarthy, Tigar and the prosecutors obviously needed and wanted the transcript of the 1931 trial. Surprisingly it was not in the files at either the District Court or the Seventh Circuit Court of Appeals (where the conviction was appealed). The Litigation Section found it in the archives of the Treasury Department. Parenthetically, that was how the Treasury Department people got involved in the trial.

MacCarthy and Tigar filed several appropriate and helpful pre-trial motions, (none of which were filed in the original trial) in the main aimed at keeping out illegal and improper information. They also carefully drafted their proposed jury instructions, including "theory of the case" instructions, which Judge Marshall gave. Again this was not done by the original trial lawyers.

During the trial Judge Marshall took a recess or as we non-lawyers would call it, a break. No doubt to keep some of the audience in their seats, he, the jury being excused for the recess, favorably commented on the trial. He suggested the lawyering was outstanding and in particular praised MacCarthy's cross-examination of the snitch Fred Reis, as being the best he had ever seen.

MacCarthy and Tigar turned up and used interesting information that was not used in the 1931 trial.

A Palm Island Florida neighbor was upset with the noise at Capone's parties. The neighbor happened to be a close friend of President Hoover, to whom he complained and from whom he asked that something be done. This prompted President Hoover to order the Treasury people to "get Capone".

Also the defense, in particular MacCarthy on cross-examination, brought out the fact that Fred Reis, who had an exceptional and irrational fear of bugs, was purposely put in a bug infested downstate Illinois jail. After suffering for a week he made the statements the prosecutors wanted him to make.

The jury deliberated for over three hours. Their verdict was announced at a Litigation Section dance and cocktail party that evening. The jury found Al Capone not guilty on all counts. The verdict was met with thunderous applause. Within days major newspapers throughout Europe and even some in the states, carried lead articles about the acquittal.

———

I would love to know what the odds were on the day I was born that I would have the success I have had in my life, or that I would raise such a wonderful family. There I was, the firstborn child of a man whose father was a convicted felon who served time in a county jail in Chicago and federal prison in the Washington state for income tax evasion and then was dubbed Public Enemy #3. His partner, my uncle Al Capone, served seven-and-a-half years in Alcatraz and other prisons for income tax evasion, and was known world wide as Public Enemy #1. As if this weren't enough, I was raised in the shadow of my father's pain due to his family legacy, and my mother was never equipped to be a wife or a mother.

In the end, I survived the Capone legacy. I have been happily married to my best friend since 1963; I am a mother to four and a grandmother to fourteen; and I became a successful, legitimate businesswoman in Minnesota.

What I have shared with you here are many family stories, secrets, and photographs never known or seen by anyone outside of our family. I even threw in a few recipes for the favorite dishes Al asked his mother to prepare for him—meals I often shared with him.

This has been a difficult book for me to write for a number of reasons, the foremost being the pain these memories have awakened. I continued with it because no one else could. I did it for my children, grandchildren, and history.

It is my hope that you've seen from my story a glimpse of the heart of the Capones. Perhaps, too, you've seen courage and determination in my story and those of my family members. We had numerous setbacks and heartbreaks, but I truly believe I have a guardian angel that kept whispering in my ear. Fortunately, I listened.

My purpose for writing this book is not to try to change anyone's opinion of my uncle Al Capone or gloss over any of the documented incidents related to him or the Outfit. My intent, instead, is three-fold: first, to educate the public on another side of my uncle, a man who had a family, a heart, and a sense of purpose; second, to correct some of the errors written about him, corrections that could only come from a family member's point of view; and third, to show that there has not been a single person carrying Capone blood that has been a detriment to society. It is my hope that this last purpose will give some meaning to my father's all-too-brief life but enduring legacy—a legacy that lives in me and my family.

The books and movies about Al Capone document and dramatize the crimes, the influence, and the "sit downs" with the crime bosses, but now you know the man behind the infamy, the man I called "Uncle Al."

———

During all these years, I have spoken with many people who related personal accounts of interacting with Al during his era. I will tell you that I never met anyone who interacted with him outside of his business who was afraid or spoke unkindly of him. He was always the first person to offer help if someone needed it.

Take my uncle's chef, Pepozek DiBuono. After Al was sentenced for income tax evasion, Al gave him some money and said, "Peppe, I want you to open your own restaurant so that other people can enjoy your cooking." The original restaurant was a small room, no more than ten tables covered with red checked oilcloths, a blackboard on the wall by the door where the offerings of the day were written in chalk, and a sign outside that read: Taylor Street Tap. We always called it Peppe's. After Peppe died, we called it Sammy's after his son who took over.

Sammy's has expanded over the years and is now called Tufano's, after Sammy's mother and Peppe's grandson now runs it. This restaurant has been operating for close to seventy years, providing the DiBuono family with their livelihood. It is a local landmark to this day. Many years after the original loan, Peppe tried to give the money back to Al's mother, but she refused it. She considered the DiBuonos, *goombas*, family, and insisted they owed her nothing.

And Al's kindness extended beyond friends of the family, too. I was speaking to a writer a couple of years ago about the possibility of her helping me write my book. When I told her who I was, she hesitated for a minute and then started to laugh. Her grandfather had told her a story about my uncle.

Her grandfather had two sisters who were spinster schoolteachers. In the late 20s they saved their money for a trip to see the Windy City. Their goal was to visit the museums and go to the theatre. Shortly after they arrived in the city, a tire blew out on their car. The two got out, and as they stood looking at it and wondering what to do, a black limousine pulled up alongside them. The man in the back seat rolled down his window and asked, "Do you ladies need help?" Of course their reply was that they did, and the man told his driver to change the tire for them.

While the driver did his work, the three had a conversation. The sisters told the gentleman where they were from, and what they wanted to see while in the big city. He presented the ladies with his business card: "Al Brown, Furniture Dealer." He told them, "If you ladies need anything while you are in Chicago, give me a call."

The sisters had a wonderful time, but on the last day after they returned from an outing, they discovered that the cash they had hidden in their room had been stolen. Women of that day never carried much cash on their person. They didn't know what to do, as they needed that cash to pay the hotel bill and buy gas for the trip home.

They decided to call Mr. Brown. "Mr. Brown, can we borrow $100? We promise to repay you as soon as we get back to Sioux Falls."

Mr. Brown asked which hotel they were in and how much money they lost. He then said, "Please stay in your room and I will send someone over right away."

About ten minutes later, there was a knock on the door. When the ladies asked who was there, the voice replied, "The hotel manager, ma'am."

When they opened the door, the hotel manager stood there with a wide-eyed look on his face.

He handed them a stack of cash and murmured in awe, "Why didn't you tell me that you were friends of Al Capone?"

Family Photographs

This picture was taken in from of 7244 S. Prairie Ave. My dad, Ralph
Gabriel, is sitting on the horse and my aunt Mafalda (Maffie)
is standing alongside 1923.

Al Capone and his brother Albert (uncle Bites) in Miami 1940

Al Capone and niece Dolores Maritote

Al Capone and friend in Mercer Wisconsin 1945

Al Capone and his mother Theresa Miami 1946.

Al Capone and Larry Fels Chicago 1945

This is one of the earliest photographs of Al Capone. It was taken the day he graduated high school and before he had the scars on his face. He is sitting in front of the pool hall where his father, sitting next to Al, died of a massive heart attack in 1920. Look at the reflection in the window and you will see the apartment building across the street where they lived. The woman standing on the balcony is Al's mother Theresa holding my father who was just a month old. The man standing is Vincenzo Raiola. 1917.

Albert (uncle Bites) Capone, Chicago 1922

This is the only photograph in existence where Al Capone has a pistol in his hand. On the back of the picture my grandmother wrote "Al plays cops & robbers while hiding out in Wisconsin. 1925

In this image taken while on a hunting trip to Wisconsin, my
dad is blindfolded and Al, my grandfather and friends hold
shotguns pointing at my dad.

Albert, Theresa, Ralph Capone in Miami 1935 after Ralph's release from
prison. Albert was living in Miami to help Mae with Sonny.

Deirdre Capone sitting on Al Capone's lap as he plays Santa.

Ralph Capone Sr and Ralph Capone Jr 1922 Chicago

1915 New York, my grandfather Ralph practicing his
'poker face' in three way mirror

My grandfather teaching me to dance in Mercer
summer of 1951 after my father died.

Summer 1940 Ralph Capone holding Deirdre Capone
in Chicago at Prairie Avenue home.

Ralph Gabriel Capone, Deirdre Capone, Elizabeth (Betty) Capone

This photograph of my grandfather was in his prison file.

Grandfather Ralph Capone with his mother Theresa Capone 1935
Miami after Ralph's release from prison for income tax evasion.

My father Ralph Gabriel Capone in Florida 1935.

This photograph of Theresa Capone was given to Al when he was in
prison. You will see that she signed it to "dear son, love Mother"

Picture of Sonny Capone and his mother Mae Capone in front
of their restaurant in Miami, *The Grotto* 1953.

Mathew (uncle Matty) Capone Miami 1967

Appendix

Here is how Johnny Chase described one of the most incredible escapes in history: This is an exact copy of a letter that he sent to a "Sister Pat". He wrote this on April 27, 1970. The copy I have is in his own handwriting. I got it from Father Joseph M. Clark's personal achieves with permission.

"From January 1934 to August 1934, Warden James A. Johnston made frequent trips to other prisons in the United States, both Federal, and State penitentiaries, studying the procedures of these prisons.

From his personal study and observations of these State and Federal prisons, he and his staff selected rules and regulation the deemed most suitable for Alcatraz.

Among those rules selected was the "Silent System" in force at the time at 'Stillwater Penitentiary" in Minnesota.

The Silent System as it was enforced at Alcatraz, seemed to be the nucleus of all the unrest, trouble, and violence that happened on Alcatraz.

Each man upon entering Alcatraz was given a number and from the moment he received his number his identity was lost. He became that number. He was addressed by that number. He answered to that number. All papers concerning him were identified by that number. His mail, clothes, shoes, cell, place of work, were located through that number. It was a number he would remember to the day of his death.

The silent system forbade the inmate to talk while in the cell, cell house, dining room, or wherever the inmates came to gather, while in the main buildings, like shower rooms, clothing room, sick call, or court call.

After a new inmate was in Alcatraz a few days he became somewhat proficient in sign language. Most every one communicated with their hands.

Alcatraz was populated with convicts from other Federal prisons. These convicts were those who were trouble-makers in the other prisons, or men who had tried to escape, and those who did escape and later got caught.

When Warden Johnston toured the other Penitentiaries, he also went through the files on all those inmates already selected to go to Alcatraz, when it officially opens.

Due to the fact that Alcatraz was to be populated with escape artists, Warden Johnston also saw to it that many of these men, whose record, and files also revealed that they were informers, were to be the first men to go to Alcatraz.

His, and the Federal Bureau of Prisons purpose was to have these men while at Alcatraz, to point out the "weak-spots" as they recognized them. And to become informers on those convicts contemplating escape, either by word, or by actions.

Among these informers sent to Alcatraz was Roy Gardener, number 110, an escape artist par excellence, turned informer. He arrived among the very first to be sent to Alcatraz on Sept. 2nd 1934.

Roy Gardener was notorious for his many escapes. He escaped from U. S. Marshall's, from trains, from penitentiaries. These escapes made by Gardener in the 1920's are legend, colorful, and daring.

Roy Gardener would be taken from his cell, while all the other inmates were locked up. (All cells in Alcatraz were single cells, that is; one man to a cell) and interrogated as to what the other convicts were talking about in relation to the Security of the Island, escapes and so forth.

Roy Gardener would sometimes be taken outside the cell house and out upon the cat-walks where he would point out to the officials possible escape routes.

These would be promptly reinforced, barb-wired, or completely concreted as the condition demanded. One of the routes he caused to be sealed up with concrete was the tunnel containing pipe lines to the dock area. Another was the windows over the power-house. Here he suggested a tower be erected to control any possible approach by way of the laundry roof.

The convict population of Alcatraz at this time was unaware of these trips by Gardener, or of Gardener to be the informer he was until most of the avenues of escape were sealed off. Then, those men who knew the true Gardener were beginning to be transferred to Alcatraz.

Most of Gardener's stooling and informing became known when a guard was reprimanded by the Warden for disobeying a suggestion put to him by Roy Gardener.

Gardener actually man-handled this guard. The guard made out a "shot" (disciplinary report) on Gardener and presented it to his superiors for processing.

Instead of Gardener being punished, the Warden called the guard in "on the carpet" removed him from the supervision of Gardener and the other man in the mat shop, and given another duty in the front office where he rarely came into contact with the inmates. But this guard did expose what Gardener, and others were doing, to some of the inmates.

Meanwhile the convicts were beginning to tighten up. Becoming wary. Talking only to those few fellow inmates they knew before coming to Alcatraz. And on occasion with a few other inmates with whom it was almost necessary in order to gain information pertinent to their schemes and plots, of which there were many.

I was one of those few, who had, or was, able to gather information needed for the several plots being in the making at about the time I was in Alcatraz for a year.

I was a former rum runner, and knew the Bay Waters pretty well. On top of this I used to live in the Bay Area for many years and knew all the roads to travel. The best places to hide, and possible meeting places.

As a matter of fact I was in the rare position of being the only person knowing about three plots in formation going on at the same time, at Alcatraz!

Although some of the convicts in one plot knew personally other inmates in the other plots, each only knew the details of the plot he was considered "in" on. They being the type of men , they all were, inside or outside, jail-break, or bank robbery, they will not talk about the "caper" they are about to execute, with anyone other than those participating in that caper.

I was considered a participant in practically all 3 plots by virtue of my associates on the outside. And because of my knowledge of the Bay waters, the Bay area, and escape routes (roads) to avoid possible road-blocks, etc.

Then again I was working in the machine shop, a place where the essentials that are needed in most any escape are either gotten, or made.

In the spring of 1937 Ralph Roe, (#260) and Ted Cole, (#258), approached me as to the feasibility of swimming ashore.

The talks at these times were limited, and a good deal of the talk was "feeling out" the other guy, as to his thoughts and knowledge of leaving the island.

These talks took place as we walked in the yard. Or as we managed to get behind one another in sick call line, bath line, or standing beside one another on a "call-out". In general, wherever the opportunity came or presented itself, we would exchange views and thoughts pertaining to the tides, their speed, and the drift towards or away from shore. Which was the best chance to take? Should we go with the incoming tide or the out-going tide? Which way the water was traveling and when was it moving towards the ocean or in across the Bay towards Berkeley. How fast did the tide flow? How long a start would be needed? What would be needed and how would they get it?

After several meetings it was generally agreed upon that the best time would be in the winter months when the fog was thickest, like it was the previous January, even though the risk was greater, because of the cold, low tides and faster currents.

Ralph Roe worked in the shop adjoining the machine shop where I (Johnny Chase) worked. To this shop, (the mat shop) I had access. When there were repairs to be done I would manage to go accompanied by a guard. These jobs would be purposefully created at times by jamming the machines so they would break down and not perform.

When the machine or the die that cuts the segments of rubber for the mats would not perform, I and another machinist would go over with a guard and make the necessary replacements or repairs. At these times we would communicate.

Ted Cole worked on what was known as the Labor Crew. This crew, was headquartered for calls through our shop, and their guard used our shops telephone to receive calls.

Ted Cole had just come out of the "hole". The jobs on the Labor Crew were considered heavy work and were assigned as a disciplinary measure.

Ted would always manage to have something break, or find something to be brought into the machine shop, or to the blacksmith shop, which was also in the same area and under the same supervisor as was the machine shop.

In this shop, officially called the "Blacksmith Shop" eight men worked. The officer in charge was Joe Steere. His detail was known as the "Blacksmith and mat shop detail."

On top of the roof of the building that housed these shops, was a guards tower and "cat walk". This guard in the tower commanded a clear view of all the shops in the work area. No convict could pass out of a shop door without first being "cleared" by the shop foreman, to the Tower Guard. This was generally done by the guard stepping outside the door and waving his arm toward the tower guard. Then, the shop foreman would beckon to the inmate to come out. He would then point his arm and finger toward the shop indicating where he was sending the convict. The tower guard usually gave the O.K. Most of the time the shop foreman, would telephone the tower guard and tell him that he was sending a man to a certain shop, then come out with the inmate and wave the clearance to the tower guard.

If a convict stepped outside one of the doors without an okay, the guard, (so we were told) would shoot to kill. Several convicts stepped outside in the two years I worked in that area. Immediately the guard would aim his rifle at the convict and bellow a command to "get back in there!

In the spring of 1937 there were several inmates preparing themselves physically for making a try at swimming off Alcatraz toward shore.

Two of these men were Ralph Roe (#260) and Theodore Cole (#258). Both of these men were from Oklahoma. Ralph was about 28 or 29 years old. He was a good athlete and kept himself physically fit. Ted Cole was about 23 years old, quick tempered with a low boiling point, and always in good shape. Ted Cole went to prison the first time when he was 17 years old. He escaped but was recaptured. While waiting in the jail at Tulsa to be returned to McAlester penitentiary he killed his cell mate.

When Cole was returned to McAlester, he again escaped. This time he kidnapped a farmer and forced him to drive him into Texas. There he was apprehended and sentenced to 50 years under the Lindbergh Kidnap law. He was brought to Alcatraz along with Ralph Roe.

Ralph Roe was also from Oklahoma, from Muskagee, Oklahoma. Ralph has been in and out of prisons since he was 20 years old. In 1934, he escaped from McAlester and robbed the Farmers Bank in Sulphur, Oklahoma. He got a large amount of money which was never recovered. He was sentenced to a federal prison for robbing a Federal Reserve System bank.

Ralph Roe and Ted Cole came to me with one of their plans to escape. They asked questions and we discussed what needed to be done to be successful.

We talked, and what evolved from these talks was a very careful plan that took months to develop. It included the confidence of one other person besides myself and Ralph and Ted. This fellows' name was Bartlett (#239) who was the next inmate to arrive at Alcatraz after I did.

Ralph and Ted arrived in October 1935.

The tentative route of escape they finally agreed upon was through the barred windows of the Blacksmith Shop, followed by a drop down to the "cat walk" that ran alongside the building and continued around the building to the fog horn located on the northwest end of the Island. This "cat walk" was fenced in by a cyclone fence on the Bay side, the building on the Island side, and barbed wire across the top.

About 25 to 35 feet from the window they intended to go through was a gate in the fence. This gate was closed and had a chain wrapped around it, with a huge padlock holding it in place. The first plans that developed were to pass thru this gate, drop into the water, and swim out to a small island where another fog horn was located. This fog horn worked with the rise and fall of the tide. It wasn't a fog horn so much, but it was a bell, and around this bell were bell rings suspended in such a way that every time the buoy would move the ringers would strike the bell.

Anyway, one of the ideas was to have a boat come thru the fog on an appointed day and, being guided by the fog horn, then the bell buoy, this boat would come to the small island that sits about 50 feet away from Alcatraz proper.

To get through the gate in the fence they would need something to twist the lock until it broke. A stillson wrench or a stout steel bar would easily do this.

Getting out of the Blacksmith shop would be a simple matter. We had hack-saw blades and although we could only use these blades under the eyes of the officer, we had some "planted" that the guard wasn't aware of. The biggest obstacle was the water itself. The water was always cold. If one had to stay in it any length of time he would need to prepare for that.

To this end we had plenty of grease. The machines all needed grease for the bearings, and there were two 5 gallon cans of grease in the shop. One was for grease guns, the other for grease cups.

As we talked and discussed the escape over the weeks and months, we covered all aspects, including where to land. Then we had to have clothes ready or to break into some place like the barracks over at Fort Baker. I was familiar with the docks there, the building that housed the "stores", and the buildings that the soldiers lived in.

All this with the different roads into and out of Marin County we discussed over, and over, time, after time with each other.

We needed money and weapons, and someone came up with the idea of using one gallon cans for water wings. This was a very good suggestion and it is the one item that makes me believe that Ralph and Ted really made it ashore, and away. Before they left, they put sharp daggers in the cans, (one for each man) and all the money that they could gather together.

They had close to $400 most of it belonging to Capone (#85).

Al Capone got into a swindle shortly before the escape plan began to develop. Capone had some money sent into the prison for him, which he divided into several batches of $500 hidden in different parts of the island where it was accessible to inmates who he trusted.

Somehow Capone was "tripped up" by one of his "trustworthy friends", Montgomery (#67), who informed the officials that Capone had some money planted in the Renovating Plant.

One of the fellows who had access to another $500 took it all for himself. This $500, or what was left of it, about $375 was given to Ralph and Ted just before they left. I saw them put the money into one of the cans then take it out and divide it, putting half in each. So each had half of the $375 plus some other money, plus the dagger made from files. These daggers were as sharp as a razor and made of tempered steel. I was told later that the cans were found on the beach near Ft. Baker, but there was no mention of the money or weapons.

During the months before the actual escape, there were many things to be done, including conditioning their bodies for the icy cold waters.

To this end, neither one of them wore any clothing except the "coveralls" they had to wear. In this way they conditioned themselves to withstand the cold winds, the rain, and the fogs as they walked the island.

They always cavorted and played around with water. In the shop they would have someone throw buckets of cold water on them. The clothes got very wet and they would keep them on as long as they could before the guard made them change. They always showered in cold water.

Out in the yard at recreation periods they went through all the strenuous exercises that were permissible. They played hand-ball, did push-ups, wrestled and took fast walks back and forth in the yard for long lengths of time.

They drank nothing hot. Always cold water. And again there was other "conditioning" to do. This was a conditioning of all those who were close to the Blacksmith shop. So that on the day they were to leave, every move would not be unusual or alert convict, or guard, that something was about to happen.

To this end we would get the guard used to "missing" one of us at count call, then after a while to miss two.

To do this, one of us would go over to the locker that Joe Steere kept things in, to which we had keys made from an impression of his. One would open it just as Joe Steere was about to count his men, and close the door behind him. This locker would just about hold one man, and he had to squeeze into it.

When the officer (Steere) would just about be ready to telephone in, that he was short a man, one of us would call him out of sight of the locker. The fellow in it would come out and then Steere would "see him" check him off the count sheet, then call in his "count" as being "okay" to the control room.

This hiding out got to be quite a game. At first the officer became concerned, then gradually he became accustomed to hunting down one or two of us, when we would keep out of his sight by hiding in the locker, or moving from one shop to the other. We could move back and forth between the blacksmith shop, the tinsmith shop and the mat shop by an areaway which was out of sight by the tower.

As the months passed, I worked myself into sitting in the guards' chair, at his desk. Here he kept his count sheet, which he was supposed to check-off every ½ hour, and every 2 hours he was supposed to call the control room.

Joe Steere got to the point where he became lax. He liked to work at jobs, being a pretty good mechanic and a good electrician. So he sometimes neglected to check off his men at the ½ hour, waiting till he had to "call in" his count at 9:30 and 11:00 in the mornings and at 2:30 and 3:30 in the afternoon.

While I sat at his desk, and he came in, I would ask sometimes, 'Everybody accounted for?' He would then say, 'Okay, John, check 'em off.' This I would do by putting check marks in the squares indicating the time in ½ hours, alongside each name and number.

We would also make excuses to have him "pass" one of us over to the electric shop at about "count time", around the time he would have to call the control room. These trips paid off handsomely when Ralph and Ted left.

But in the meantime we started cutting the bars because the crew that went around testing the bars by hitting them with rubber hammers to see if they were firm and not sawed had made the tests in our shops. From the method they used, and from the length of time between tests, we figured it would be safe to cut the bars almost through, then put putty in the saw-cut to hide the fact that they were cut. Long before we cut the bars, we began knocking out the glass in the windows, which were small squares about 6 X 8 inches. Each time we knocked out a pane of glass (accidentally of course) we would then insert a piece of wood in place of the glass. This piece was held in place by twisting a lath-like piece of wood fastened in the middle. This lath-like piece when twisted horizontally would wedge against the steel frame and hold fast.

Of all the men that worked in these shops, it was amazing that the officials were not informed, or even alerted by the preparations that seemed so obvious. Although, after the bars were cut, I don't believe more than 4 of us knew they were ready to be twisted out.

Next we began to get the guard on the tower used to answering the phone. We would dial his number (which was 06) when Joe Steere was over in the mat shop. At these times we would watch the tower guard, and when he was about to leave the tower to make his round, over the roof-top, looking around and down, we would call his number. He would then go back into the tower and answer the phone. Sometimes we would not talk and he would say "hello" a few times, then hang up, sit awhile expecting it to ring again, then go out. Sometimes we would ring a second time and then when he answered we would ask him if he could see Joe Steere around, not giving him a name or indicating who was calling. Sometimes we asked him to locate the electrician, or if the truck was in the area, anything to keep him a few more minutes in the tower.

Finally the winter months came. In December 1937 there were some dense fogs.

And to make things more exciting, one of the signs that we were watching for came off on schedule. We heard through a fellow inmate by the name of Amos, who came from Oklahoma, that he had been discharged some months before and had things to do on the outside for several Oklahomans who were in Alcatraz.

When he left, the pre-arranged signal was for him to ride the "*Eureka*" ferry boat from Sausalito at the time in the morning this boat always passed the island on the west side. He had to make sure the *Eureka* passed on the west side in order for us to see it. In order to make sure, he had to know which way the tide was running out the Gate. These boats always went on the side of Alcatraz that would make the ferry boat safe from crashing onto the Island if something went wrong as the ferry was passing the "Rock".

The signal was for Amos to stand alone on the front of the "*Eureka*" whether it be rainy or foggy. We noticed while watching the ferry boats pass the Rock shuttling back and forth between Sausalito and San Francisco, that almost no one stood out on front of the boat. This was because it was so cold and windy.

One morning, sure enough, there was a guy standing out there on the Eureka! (There were many other ferry boats shuttling back and forth, but our boat was the Eureka.) To be sure that it was no fluke, Amos was to stand out there with only a suit coat on and no hat. He was to remain on the boat while in San Francisco, and be on it as it passed coming back toward Sausalito. And there he was! Our signal was simply dropping a white pillow case out the window at the end of a small cord. This white pillow case was seen and acknowledged by Amos as the boat went by.

Finally, on December 16 or 17· both Ralph and Ted were ready. The day before they left was a good day, but they couldn't make up their minds to go.

The day was good and foggy. I said, 'Two days like today and yesterday, are very rare. You'll never get fogs as dense as these'.

So, as planned, as soon as Joe Steere made his count and reported to the control room that the count was okay, Ralph and Ted stripped off their clothes. Joe Steere left the shop with Bartlett; it had been prearranged for Bartlett to ask to go to the electric shop.

After stripping off their clothing, they smeared themselves with all the grease from the two 5 gallon cans. They had grease all over them good and thick; they took their 1 gallon cans, which were tied together like water wings, and their big stillson wrench. They were all ready to go out the window! The bars were jerked out! They both shook hands with me. Everybody else was working at their jobs.

When they left it was 9:40 a.m. They went through the window without seemingly touching the sides! I went over where I could command a view of the tower and the outside entrance of our shop.

Slim Bartlett came back, and with him was Joe Steere. It was about 10 a.m. and time for the guard to check his men.

When Joe left for the mat shop again I had to call the tower, because "Betty Boop", the guard, was fixing to leave. He came back and answered the call, then waited. This guards' name was Cokenaur; we had nick-named him Betty-Boop.

Joe Steere came back in and was trying to find his two men. Although he didn't ask any questions I could see that he was concerned.

No one attempted to fix the window where Ralph and Ted went out. Luckily, Joe Steere didn't look for an opening because it looked huge compared to the small frames!

As usual Joe Steere had not made any checks against the men's names and numbers on his 9:30 count sheet.

By 10:45 Joe was really concerned now. One of the men working in the machine shop asked me, "Have those fellows gone?" I answered 'they've been gone now for over an hour.'

Finally Joe Steere had made up his mind that he had lost two men and he started to take the telephone down to dial the control room. I spoke up and said, 'Mr. Steere, you had better check your count sheet before you call in.'

He came over, picked up the count sheet and looked at it.

I told him, 'you know Joe, the first thing the Captain will do when he comes in will be to pick up the count sheet to see when you checked them off last, and will want to know why you didn't do it every half hour?'

So Joe Steere checked everybody in for all the squares, indicating everyone was there at 9:30, 10:00, 10:30 and now at 11 a.m. he picks up the telephone and tells the control room he was short two men!

The whistles blew, horns and sirens moaned out like hound dogs. "Whineholt", the Captain, rushed in and, sure enough, the first thing he did was to pick up the count sheet and check it. Then he and the Deputy Warden asked Joe when he saw them last. Joe said, 'sometime between 10:30 and 11:00.'

The Captain sent out an alarm to the Coast Guard. The boats were converging below us, coming in close, in the fog, then backing out.

The other convicts were all moving into the cell house, each detail with extra guards walking with them. Finally, we are all locked up.

Ralph and Ted had an hour and 25 minute head start. The report to the searchers was that they had been missing for about 15 minutes. This gave Ralph and Ted a free area from the search boats, because they concentrated their search close to the Island, figuring it would take more than 15 minutes to get any distance away.

It was very cold and the fog was thick. The whole population of Alcatraz was electrified. After we were all secured in our cells, the full custodial force searched the work area, hoping to find Ralph and Ted hiding somewhere inside.

When the F.B.I. arrived they commandeered the island's boat and made an exhaustive search of all the small inlets (like caves) that had been carved into the island by the tides and the western winds over the years.

Two days later, after the bars were welded back in place, and we were back on the job, the F.B.I. agents were still searching. I looked out the window as the boat full of agents (F.B.I.) came toward where the window was located. As the boat eased in toward the island, one of the F.B.I. men trained his binoculars at the window I was looking out. I thumbed my nose at him.

Two months later, I was taken from Alcatraz to New York City to appear at a trial, and also before the Grand Jury. While waiting in the custody of the F.B.I. in the Federal Bldg in Foley Square, many agents came to where I was under guard on the 30th floor. One of them looked at me and put his thumb to his nose! I put my two hands to my eyes as though I was holding a pair of binoculars.

The agent laughed and said, 'We know each other!'

I then asked him why they didn't question me about the escape. They had called out everyone else who worked in those shops and questioned them, but not me.

The agent said they didn't have any confidence in me or my answers because they still remembered Chicago.

During the 10 days after the escape, the F.B.I. were constantly at my brother's home in Sausalito, expecting Ralph and Ted to show up there. So someone, or perhaps several inmates, must have told the F.B.I. during questioning that "Ralph, Ted, and I were always together."

From all I can gather, I would say that Ralph and Ted did make land and were in good shape. They had planned for everything that could conceivably happen and had prepared for it.

I was informed that the gallon cans were found. But I never heard anyone mention the finding of any money, or the daggers that were in them. Over the many years, I never mentioned these cans, until one day I did, to an inmate named Chuck Cole (#535).

From the many talks I had with Ralph Roe and Ted Cole, the briefings on escape routes, hiding places and the importance of committing no crimes, I was convinced that if they did make shore, they also made freedom, as they envisioned what needed to be done to accomplish their freedom. And the finding of the cans minus the contents, leaves little doubt, but what they did escape." -Johnny Chase

Al Capone Quotes

- "Hell, it's a business... All I do is supply a public demand. I do it in the best and least harmful way I can. I can't change the conditions. I just meet them without backing up."

- "Don't get the idea I'm one of those goddam radicals. Don't get the idea I'm knocking the American system."

- "I give the public what it wants. I never had to send out high-pressure salesmen. I could never meet the demand."

- "When I sell liquor, they call it bootlegging. When my patrons serve it on silver trays on Lake Shore Drive, they call it hospitality."

- "If machines are going to take jobs away from the worker, then he will need to find something else to do. Perhaps he'll get back to the soil. But we must care for him during the period of change. We must keep him away from Red literature, Red ruses; we must see that his mind remains healthy."

- "I'll go as deep in my pockets as any man to help any guy that needs help. I can't stand to see anybody hungry or cold or helpless."

- "A crook is a crook, and there's something healthy about his frankness in the matter. But the guy who pretends he's enforcing the law and steals on his authority is a swell snake."

- "You'd be surprised if you knew some of the fellows I've got to take care of."

- Once you're in the racket, you're always in it. The parasites will trail you, begging for money and favors, and you can never get away from them no matter where you go."

- "Well, maybe he thinks that the law of self-defense, the way God looks at it, is a little broader than the law books have it."

- "I'm the boss. I'm going to continue to run things. They've been putting the roscoe on me for a good many years and I'm still healthy and happy. Don't let anybody kid you into thinking I can be run out of town. I haven't run yet and I'm not going to."

- "Deany (Dion O'Banion) was all right and he was getting along to begin with better than he had any right to expect. But like everyone else, his head got away from his hat."

- "Of course I didn't kill McSwiggin (Assistant State's Attorney William McSwiggin). Why should I? I liked the kid. Only the day before he got knocked off he was over at my place, and when he went home I gave him a bottle of Scotch for his old man. If I wanted to knock him off, I could have done it then, couldn't I? We had him on the spot."

- "It seems like I'm responsible for every crime that takes place in this country."

- "The other day a man came in here and said that he had to have $3000. If I'd give it to him, he said, he would make me the beneficiary of a $15,000 insurance policy and then kill himself. I had to have him pushed out."

- "I told them we are making a shooting gallery out of a great business and nobody is profiting by it."

- "I wanted to stop all that because I couldn't stand hearing my little kid ask why I didn't stay home. I had been living at the Hawthorne Inn for fourteen months… If it wasn't for him, I'd have said, To hell with you fellows. We'll shoot it out."

- "Things people know about amuse them. They like to laugh over them and make jokes. When a speakeasy is raided, there are a few hysterical people, but the general mass are light hearted. On the other hand, do you know any of your friends who'd go into fits of merriment if they feared being taken for a ride?"

- "It's pretty tough when a citizen with an unblemished record must be hounded from his home by the very policemen whose salaries are paid, at least in part, from the victim's pocket. You might say that every policeman in Chicago gets some of his bread and butter from the taxes I pay."

- "I'm getting sick of fellows like Hughes using me to attract glory to themselves. I never met Hughes in my life, nor have I ever even received a telephone call from him. Chase me out of Cook County? Well, he hasn't done it and he won't do it."

- "I am a property-owner and taxpayer in Chicago."

- "I'm out of the booze racket now and I wish the papers would let me alone."

- "It's hard, dangerous work, aside from any hate at all, and when a fellow works hard at any line of business he wants to go home and forget about it. He don't want to be afraid to sit near a window or an open door."

- "I have always been opposed to violence, to shootings. I have fought, yes, but fought for peace. And I believe I can take credit for the peace that now exists in the racket game in Chicago. I believe that the people can thank me for the fact that gang killings here are probably a thing of the past."

- "Why not treat our business like any other man treats his, as something to work at in the daytime and forget when he goes home at night? There's plenty of business for everybody. Why kill each other over it?"

- "Nobody was ever killed except outlaws, and the community is better off without them."

- "Today I got a letter from a woman in England. Even over there I'm known as a gorilla. She offered to pay my passage to London if I would kill some neighbors she's having a quarrel with."

- "I paid McSwiggin and I paid him plenty, and I got what I was paying for."

- "I'm sorry Hymie (Weiss) was killed, but I didn't have anything to do with it... There's enough business for all of us without killing each other like animals in the street."

- "Union members look at dues the same way they look at taxes; just something you got to pay the thieves who run things."

- "Crooked bankers who take people's hard-earned cash for stock they know is worthless would be far better clients at penal institutions than the little man who robs so that his wife and babies may live."

- "The worst type is the Big Politician who gives about half his time to covering up so that no one will know he's a thief. A hard-working crook can buy these birds by the dozens, but he hates them in his heart."

- "Graft is a byword in American life today. It is law where no law is obeyed. It is undermining this country. The honest lawmakers of any city can be counted on your fingers. I could count Chicago's on one hand."

- "A kidnapper is no better than a rat, and I don't approve of his racket because it makes the kidnapped man's wife and kiddies worry so much. I shall be glad to help Chicago in this emergency."

- "They talk about me not being legitimate. Nobody's on the legit. You know that and so do they. Nobody's really on the legit when it comes down to cases."

- "I've seen gambling houses, too--in my travels, you understand--and I never saw anyone point a gun at a man and make him go in. I've never heard of anyone being forced to go to a place to have some fun."

- "The funny part of the whole thing is that a man in this line of business has so much company. I mean his customers. If people did not want beer and wouldn't drink it, a fellow would be crazy for going around trying to sell it."

- "I violate the Prohibition law, sure. Who doesn't? The only difference is that I take more chances than the man who drinks a cocktail before dinner and a flock of highballs after it."

- "My rackets are run on strictly American lines and they are going to stay that way."

- "Some of the biggest Dry in the country buy from me and have for years, so let's stop kidding."

- All I ever did was sell beer and whiskey to our best people. All I ever did was supply a demand that was pretty popular. Why, the very guys that make my trade good are the ones that yell the loudest about me. Some of the leading judges use the stuff.

- "Nobody wanted Prohibition. This town voted six to one against it. Somebody had to throw some liquor on that thirst. Why not me?"

- "Let the worthy citizens of Chicago get their liquor the best way they can.

- I'm sick of the job. It's a thankless one and full of grief"

- "I leave with gratitude to my friends who have stood by me through this unjust ordeal, and with forgiveness for my enemies. I wish them all a Merry Christmas and Happy New Year."

- "The country wanted booze, and I organized it. Why should I be called a "public enemy"?

- "People who respect nothing dread fear. It is upon fear, therefore,
that I have built up my organization. But understand me correctly,
please. Those who work with me are afraid of nothing. Those who
work for me are kept faithful, not so much because of their pay as
because they know what might be done with them if they broke
faith."

- "I'm a business man. I've made my money supplying a popular
demand. If I break the law, my customers are as guilty as I am."

Capone Family Recipes

I have all the family recipes in my collection but for space reasons I am only including a couple here.

Grandma Theresa's Fresh Bread

This is the actual recipe for the bread Theresa Capone baked and sold in Brooklyn. Back in the days when I learned to bake this bread, the flour was fresh. In fact, if you did not use the flour within a couple of weeks, tiny bugs would appear.

large electric mixer
baking stone
2 cups scalding water
1 cake compressed or 1 envelope dry yeast
6 or 6 ½ cups flour
1 tbsp salt
2 tbsp sugar
2 tbsp butter
preheat oven to 400°

Crumble or sprinkle the yeast in ¼ cup of the water. Put the butter, sugar, and salt in the remaining water in mixing bowl. When mixture is lukewarm, add the dissolved yeast, ½ of the flour, and beat. Add the remaining flour slowly, mixing with the dough hook until mixture can no longer absorb any more flour. Or until sides of the mixing bowl are clean. Toss on a floured surface and knead with your hands until smooth and elastic. When you knead, fold edges of dough toward center, and press down and away with the heel of your hand. Put into a bowl that has been brushed with olive oil. Cover and let rise until double in size.

Grandma would find the sunniest room in the house to let the dough rise in the sun.

When doubled, cut the dough with a knife, cover, and let rise again until doubled. Divide the dough into two equal pieces and shape into oblong loaves. Put cooking stone in the bottom of the oven. Place two loaves on the stone and cook for 45 minutes until golden brown. For the traditional crispy crust of good Italian bread, cool loaves on a rack in a draft, allowing the air to circulate around them.

Grandma Theresa's Ragu

Here is a little known fact. My Aunt Maffie opened a deli on the south side of Chicago after Al Capone's death. A man who was a regular customer and loved her lasagna came into the deli one day and asked for the recipe for the sauce. Maffie gave it to him, and he used it to create the very first spaghetti sauce of the Ragu Company.

This recipe is enough for one pound of pasta. Most of the time I double it; as it ages well in the refrigerator.

2-28 oz cans of Italian tomatoes pureed
4 tbsp olive oil
6 garlic cloves chopped fine
1 medium onion cut into quarters
1 whole nutmeg
6 basil leaves of 1 tbsp dried basil
1 bulb fresh fennel
1 tsp dried oregano
pinch of salt
¼ tsp fresh ground black pepper
¼ tsp red pepper flakes

Core the fresh fennel and cut into small pieces.

Take a piece of cheesecloth and wrap it around the fennel, onion, nutmeg, and basil, forming a ball that will be lowered into the tomatoes. Heat olive oil in stock pot and add garlic. Stir until the garlic has released its flavor into the oil. Add tomatoes and fennel ball. Bring to a boil stirring slowly. Lower heat and simmer slowly uncovered. Add salt and pepper.

Cook slowly for about 3 hours. Before serving remove fennel ball and discard. This is the only time before serving that we would taste the gravy—we would do it by dipping a piece of bread into the sauce and eating the bread.

Baked Lasagna

This was one of Uncle Al's favorite dishes that his mother Theresa prepared. A generous serving of this lasagna is a meal in itself. It is best appreciated if you fast for a day before sitting down to its delectable aroma and deliciously rich taste.

1 pound lasagna macaroni
1 jar Grandma Theresa's Ragu
Filling:
2 pounds ricotta cheese
¾ cup freshly grated romano cheese
4 eggs beaten
small head parsley stems removed and heads chopped coarse
3 balls mozzarella cheese sliced thin. Do not use fresh mozzarella. I prefer scaramoza cheese but it is hard to find.

I prefer to use fresh pasta. I encourage you to make your own. If you use fresh pasta rolled thin, you do not need to cook it. If you use boxed pasta cook it according to the directions on the package but make sure it is *al dente*.

Make filling as pasta is cooking. Combine ricotta, romano, eggs and parsley in large bowl. Set aside.

To build the lasagna, cover the bottom of a rectangular lasagna pan (10 X 15 X 2) with ½ jar of sauce and completely cover that with one layer of pasta. Cover pasta with a layer of mozzarella cheese Cover mozzarella with 1/3 of the ricotta filling. Repeat sequence until you have three layers. Top with layer of pasta and one more layer of mozzarella, then cover with ½ jar of sauce. Bake at 375° for about 1 hour.

Cut into large squares and serve with heated sauce. Serves at least 9 people.

Al's Recipe for Italian Beef

The two foods I missed most after moving away from Chicago were Chicago-style hot dogs and Italian beef sandwiches. Italian beef in particular is simply not available anywhere else. But now you can make it yourself using Al Capone's recipe.

It is hard to find the giardiniera, but it is available in Italian stores and is usually labeled "Chicago-style giardiniera."

3-4 pound rump roast

6 (or more) cloves garlic

½ tsp oregano

½ tsp salt

½ tsp onion powder

¼ cup chopped parsley

¼ tsp crushed red pepper

½ tsp paprika

¼ tsp nutmeg

¼ tsp thyme

6 hard crusted rolls or a loaf of Italian bread

3 red or green peppers

¼ cup olive oil

Hot giardiniera

Preheat oven to 225°. Mix dry ingredients together. Mince garlic. Place meat into a roasting pan and sprinkle with dry ingredients evenly. Place minced garlic on top of meat. Cover roasting pan tightly with cover or foil and place in oven and cook for 6-8 hours.

Wash peppers and slice, removing seeds and stem. Fry them olive oil until limp. After cooking, remove the foil and break meat apart with a fork. Pile on bread and top with fried peppers and hot giardiniera.

Yummy! Serves 6.

Mob Cookies

I call this recipe "Mob Cookies" because when my grandmother Theresa baked them and Al took them to his headquarters, all the boys raved about how much they loved them.

5 cups of flour

4 tbsp baking powder

1 cup sugar

½ cup butter

1 tbsp vanilla

4 eggs

Beat eggs and add sugar, butter, and vanilla. Sift together 2 cups of flour with baking powder. Add dry to wet ingredients and mix. Ad another 2 cups of flour gradually. Put on floured surface and knead, adding more flour until dough does not stick to your hands.

Slice dough, roll out, and cut into desired shapes. Bake on greased cookie sheet at 375° for about 12 minutes until golden.

Walnut Sauce

This was another of Al's favorite recipes.

1 pound spaghetti cooked al dente and drained well

6 large cloves fresh garlic chopped

1 ½ - 2 cups Italian extra virgin olive oil

1 cup chopped walnuts

1 cup chopped Italian parsley heads, stems removed

1 tsp crushed red pepper

pinch of salt

freshly ground black pepper to taste

Heat the olive oil in a saucepan over low heat. Add chopped garlic and walnuts and cook until garlic begins to take on color of walnuts. Add parsley and red pepper. Toss spaghetti in sauce until well covered. Add salt and pepper. Serve immediately.

Chicken and noodles

5 lb chicken

6 chicken feet, cleaned

veal bone, optional

½ cup each onion & celery chopped

2 eggs

1 1/3 cup flour (about)

½ tsp salt

Stock:

In a kettle large enough to hold the chicken, put the veal bone, chicken feet, seasoning and vegetables. Add 3 quarts cold water. Bring to a boil over medium heat. Turn to a simmer and cook one hour. Add the chicken and cover and simmer slowly until the chicken is tender, about 2 hours.

Noodles:

Beat the eggs slightly and add salt and enough flour slowly to make a stiff dough. Knead well and let stand covered ½ hour. Roll out very thin. It must not be the least bit sticky and not so dry that it is brittle.

Fold into a tight roll and cut into 8-inch strips. Unroll strips and place them one on top of the other. Now cut these long strips crosswise into medium noodles about a ¼ inch wide.

Toss them lightly with your fingers to separate well and spread them out on the board to dry for at least 1 hour.

When chicken is finished cooking, remove the chicken feet and veal bone and discard. Place the chicken in a pan and let cool, then remove all the meat from the bones. Bring the liquid in the kettle to a boil. (Today I skim the fat off the top of the broth, but back then we didn't.) Drop the noodles by the handfuls into boiling liquid for 5 minutes. Remove from heat and add the chicken meat back into the soup.

Serve. Yummy!

Al Capone's Biscotti

3 cups flour

1 cup sugar

½ cup butter

3 tsp baking powder

½ tsp salt

3 eggs

2 ounces anisette

Preheat oven to 350°. Cream butter with sugar. Beat well. Add eggs one at a time, beating well.

Mix all dry ingredients together and sift into creamed ingredients. Add the anisette and mix well again.

Shape into 4 loaves and bake on a lightly greased cookie sheet for 35 minutes.

Remove from oven and place on cutting board. Cut immediately into ½ inch slices. Place slices, cut side up, on the baking sheet and place in low heated oven to toast. Turn them to toast both sides. Cool and serve.

Pasta e Faggiola

Or as we said in our family "pasta fazool!"

1 lb small pasta such as ditah or ditalini
1/8 cup olive oil
2 cups grandma's tomato sauce
1 tsp salt
½ tsp black pepper
¼ tsp oregano
1 tsp garlic powder
1 2 ½ # can northern beans
1 onion chopped

Put oil in saucepan. Add onions, salt, pepper, oregano, and garlic. Add 2 cups tomato sauce. Cook for 10 minutes.

Add beans & cook slowly for ½ hour. Cook pasta, drain. Pour sauce over pasta. Add cheese and serve. Serves 4.

Old Fashioned Apple Pie

Pie crust:

2 cups flour
½ tsp salt
2/3 cup lard (I now use unsalted butter)
6 tbsp cold apple cider

Mix flour and salt together in a large bowl. Add lard and work with fingers (or mixer) until just slightly crumbly. Add cider and work quickly until it forms a ball. Add more cider if necessary. Divide ball in halves. Roll out, making two crusts.

Filling:

6 or 7 cooking apples (Granny Smith or Cortland)
1 cup sugar
1 tsp cinnamon
¼ stick butter

Preheat over to 350°. Peel and core apples then slice thin. Put into bowl adding sugar and cinnamon. Let stand for 15 minutes.

Place one crust on a 9-inch pie pan. Pile the apple mixture and dot with thin slices of butter. It should be very full.

Place second crust on top and trim excess crust around edges. Seal edges closed with a fork. Poke hole in the top crust to allow steam to escape. Place pie pan on top of a cookie sheet covered with foil. Place in preheated oven and turn up heat to 450° for 15 minutes. Reduce heat to 375° for 60 minutes. Then brush pie with a little milk and brush with granulated sugar and bake for additional 30 minutes or until the crust is golden brown.

Easter Bread

Large electric mixer with dough hook
2 cups scalded water
1 tbsp salt
1 tbsp sugar
1 cake compressed or 1 envelope dry yeast
8 cups flour
¼ cup lukewarm water
2 eggs beaten
8 raw eggs washed thoroughly
Preheat oven to 400°. Crumble or sprinkle yeast in the lukewarm water. Pour the 2 cups hot water over salt, oil and sugar in mixing bowl.

When the hot mixture turns lukewarm, add yeast water, eggs and flour gradually. When the sides of the mixing bowl become clean, turn the dough onto floured surface and knead with hands until smooth and elastic.

Put into bowl and cover and set aside to rise until double. Take dough out of bowl and divide into two equal pieces. Take one half and divide into 2 pieces. Take one of the halves and divide into three equal pieces. Take the larger piece and form into oblong loaf. Take the three pieces and roll each one into a long roll about 1½ inches thick.

Braid these pieces into braid and place it onto of the loaf starting at one end and as you work the braid up to the other end, place a raw egg (we colored our eggs) in each opening of the braid. Continue making sure to secure the braid at both ends of the loaf. Repeat with second loaf.

Bake on stone for 45 minutes or until golden brown